COREY HARRIS & J

SERIOUSLY?
NOW WHAT?!
— A SMALL BUSINESS GUIDE TO DISASTER PREPAREDNESS —

DEDICATIONS

Corey & Julie:

First and foremost, this book is dedicated to small business owners. You are the backbone of the economy. This book was written for each and every one of you. Thank you.

Corey:

I want to thank my friends and family for your support and decades of amazing experiences.

To Jesse and Courtney—You're always looking out for me and challenging me to improve myself, business, etc. Thank you. Love y'all.

To my 11th grade English teacher, Mrs. Haring—Who would have ever thought I'd write a book?

J&V - Stay frosty

Julie—Thank you! Writing this book and building our business has been a pain, but I'm glad I got to do it with you. Also, if it wasn't for you, I'd probably still be working for the man.

Special thanks to my mom, who my brother and I dubbed the "meanest mother in the world." Her tough love taught me how to be the responsible man I am today. I owe so much to her. Miss you, Mumma.

Julie:

Thank you to Carol, Ben, Mark, and Stacy. You're the family I'm so grateful for. To Colton and Kennedy—you own me and I'm grateful to be your (favorite) aunt. To Kacey—you're my favorite human being. I love each of you.

To my friends since first grade—y'all are treasures. I am thankful beyond measure for the memories that we've shared. From elementary pranks to skipping class in high school to staying connected after college. You are the best friends a girl could ask for. "Keep your fat butt out of 6th grade business."

To my co-author, Corey—I will forever be grateful that you told a story of fixing toasters during your job interview so many years ago. That was the moment I knew I needed you in my life. Not because you can fix a toaster, but because you are relentlessly you and there isn't anything you can't figure out. I leveled up that day.

To Ernie—To say you are the best mentor possible would be dismissive of all that you are. From the first time we sat at a conference room table together you changed my life. You willingly share everything you know about business, including the lessons you learned the hard way. You may be retired, but I love that I can still call you for advice and stories. You will forever be my go-to person for advice.

To my BYLR Ride-or-Dies, Stephanie, Matt, Lindsay, Amy, and Noah—Our friendship may still be considered new—but y'all are my people. Nobody cheers harder for me than the five of you, and I love you so much for that!

To the Cooks, for offering advice, for never sugarcoating your feedback, and for listening even when I hover on whining. You're what I miss most about PA. You're the friends I turn to when I need to be heard or when I want to laugh until I cry.

And finally, to my mom. I'm not sure if you'll be able to read this book from heaven, but if you can—I hope you give it five stars. I miss you daily, Mom.

INTRODUCTION

"Entrepreneurs are willing to work 80 hours a week to avoid working 40 hours a week."
— Lori Greiner, Entrepreneur

O wning a small business is hard work. It's hard in every sense: it takes time, cash, sweat, blood, and tears to start the business and often, to run it every day. It's a grind. But for those of us who are entrepreneurs, it satisfies our creative and innovative nature. For those of us who like to be in charge of our future, it's what keeps us up late at night and wakes us up early in the morning. For those of us who are risk-takers, it's worth the reward.

We had the "bright idea" to leave the corporate consulting world at the end of 2019 and into early 2020. We were both fed up with working for large companies and not being able to deliver value to the level we are capable of.

So, who are we? We are Corey Harris and Julie Traxler, and we have years of varied experience between us. Corey has an extensive background in the service industry, filling every role from dishwasher to partner. He has spent years consulting on IT projects as the business liaison performing process documentation, review, and improvements as well as training and project execution. Corey is the numbers guy on the team leading clients through reviewing their financials, creating easy to use report dashboards, and helping set financial goals. He is an expert on start-up strategies for new businesses, helping them build strong foundations and positioning them for future success.

Julie has been leading projects and change management programs in the corporate world since 2005. Her focus has primarily been on post-acquisition integrations, focusing on helping teams adjust to the challenges of being acquired. She is the communicator on the team and helps clients position themselves within their market and build out successful growth programs. Her eye for detail and building relationships helps her guide clients through improving sales, marketing, and branding strategies.

Above all, we are both planners; think of any crisis situation, and it's a guarantee we have a plan for it.

Combined, we have over 40 years of experience, from small businesses to Fortune 500 companies. We have been employees, and we have owned our own businesses. We have negotiated single-tenant lease agreements and implemented small business process improvements. We have navigated post-acquisition mergers and helped deliver global technology solutions. We have done it all.

We were doing our jobs (and doing them well), but something was missing in what we were delivering, something unfulfilling in the corporate world. The work wasn't personal, and it was rarely about the people or the mission; it was only about the money. So, in February of 2020, we decided that we were going to build our own business, focusing on helping small businesses. We both knew plenty of small businesses and were well connected with the community. Because of this, we realized there was a gap in business consulting. While many consulting firms focus on helping large businesses, there aren't many that focus only on small businesses.

We launched our business, SB PACE (**S**mall **B**usiness **P**lanning **A**dvising **C**oaching **E**xpertise) during the best time in recent history—the beginning of the COVID-19 pandemic. So, of course, two weeks in, we had to pivot our business model. With so much uncertainty, we, like most small businesses, didn't know where to focus because no one knew what the future was going to be. So, we started calling our friends and family who owned small businesses. We reached out to see what it was that we could do to help them, as so many businesses were struggling. We were talking through their struggles, what their experiences had been before and during the pandemic, and what they thought their future looked like.

We weren't pitching our business. We wanted to learn about what the rest of the small business community was experiencing. We talked to as many industries as we could across the country, from a manufacturing business in the Pacific Northwest to a professional service firm in the Southeast and everything in between. Through those conversations, this book was conceived, and you'll find those stories scattered throughout the chapters.

Here at SB PACE, we're planners. Whether it's launching a new website or surviving an onslaught of zombie hordes, we have thought about and made a plan (probably) for a way to survive it successfully. And that's what this book is all about: how to plan for and survive whatever comes your way as a business. We have taken our experience in large companies, small businesses, and post-apocalyptic disaster scenarios and wrapped it all up into one book aimed at helping you strengthen your business.

While it may seem like a lot of work—and sometimes it is—preparing and creating a plan for a crisis is worth it in the long run. Studies have been performed showing a significant return on preparation investment. The numbers vary, but the ballpark is about a $5 return for every $1 invested. You can spend a dollar or hour now to get five back in the case of an emergency. That seems like an easy choice.

How we
APPROACHED THIS BOOK

- First and foremost, this book is intended for you to read prior to any kind of crisis and therefore to have already prepared for it. You can refer back to it if you're in the middle of a disaster, but our goal is for the bulk of the work to be completed before you ever need a crisis plan.

- The book is broken down into three parts. Part I is the foundational work for defining and understanding your business and your people. Parts II and III focus on creating and successfully executing a well thought out plan. You may be tempted to skip some exercises or even chapters, but don't. Without the foundation from Part I, your plans may fall apart.

- We use the terms crisis, disaster, problem, predicament, event, etc. interchangeably throughout the book. While something may seem like a monumental crisis to some small businesses, it may be a minor annoyance to others and even an opportunity for a few. It's all about perspective, and we don't want you to think you should only be prepared for major disasters. You can prepare yourself for a growth opportunity. This book is all about being proactive.

- This book has a companion workbook with examples. It will help you complete exercises and build out your business survival plans as you read along. It's not necessary for you to complete it, but it's free, so there's no reason you shouldn't download it on our website. Look for this icon to know that you have an exercise to complete:

- The companion workbook can be found on our website at www.sbpace.com/workbook. Head on over there to download the interactive PDF workbook. While you're there, check out our blogs, and connect with us on social media.

- As you are reading the book, you may start to have realizations and epiphanies about your business. Even if there isn't an exercise that correlates, we encourage you to start writing. We have left some blank pages in the workbook for these types of realizations.

- If you're a solopreneur (you're the only employee in your business), we've added tips just for you at the end of chapters, where you may need to use an alternative approach to complete the exercises.

- Finally, there are two of us writing this book, so most of it is written using the first-person plural "we." Occasionally, we switch to first-person singular when telling a story, and when we do, we tell you whose story it is.

Let's get to work!

CONTENTS

PART III EXECUTE

Part I
PREPARE

01 THE FOUNDATION

"Chance favors the prepared mind."
— Louis Pasteur, Biologist

You know when you're watching a horror movie and think to yourself, *"Yeah, idiot. That's a great idea. Go check out that dark room all alone"*? Everyone knows what's coming next: the curious teenager gets decapitated by someone dressed as a clown. It's predictable.

Unfortunately for business owners, not all problems or impending disasters are as easy to spot. You're living in the moment and can't see the bigger picture. Just like the teen from a movie meeting an untimely demise, it's hard to tell when you are walking into a potentially disastrous scenario because you're living in the moment. So, how do you keep yourself from walking into that room all alone?

Julie:

Several years ago, I had a client who was living proof of Murphy's Law. Anything that could go wrong, did go wrong. I was helping this client through a post-deal close acquisition integration, where I was tasked to lead the effort to fold their company into the larger entity. It seemed like every week brought on some new disaster no one had planned for: everything from exploding sewer pipes, to animals dying in the ceiling in the heat of a Midwest summer, to an employee drug ring getting busted during the night shift. Everything.

There was one particular disaster that was extremely problematic for the client: they had an incident with the sprinkler system. That would be a problem for any business, but this client distributed food, which meant they had a section in their warehouse that was a giant freezer. One evening the sprinkler started going off in that freezer for no reason, and nobody working at the time knew how to turn it off. NOBODY. And...this happened around 1:00 AM.

So, now this client had their night crew, whose only job normally is to pull groceries, trying to perform maintenance on a sprinkler system while simultaneously calling every person who could possibly turn off the system. Of course, everyone they called was asleep because they worked during normal business hours. By the time they figured out how to turn off the sprinkler system, the freezer had transformed into a hockey rink.

Do you have any idea how difficult it is to pull cases of groceries when the floor is a sheet of ice? It's impossible. Instead of filling customer orders, the night crew spent their shift swinging hammers to clear the ice off of the floor. No one thought it was necessary to train the night shift how to work the sprinklers since the sprinklers generally only go off when there's a fire...and if there were a fire, there would be bigger problems to worry about.

It seems that most preparedness plans emerge either from firsthand experience or from witnessing a disaster elsewhere rather than from a proactive approach to mitigating a potential problem. This warehouse had an emergency plan for tornadoes, not because they had been hit by one in the past but because they were located in the Midwest where tornadoes are common. That makes sense. But the warehouse managers didn't train all shifts on how to maintain the sprinklers. Why would they? It isn't common for sprinklers to go off randomly. We are certain that to this very day, new employees are trained on how to work the sprinklers. They probably ask, "why do I need to know this?" and get the response, "Well, this one summer years ago...."

One would assume that most businesses have a plan for obvious potential disasters; however, we have found most businesses don't, or they only have one when required to by their local government (such as having an annual fire drill, for example). Noah Pines of the Ross and Pines Law Firm said it best during an interview with us: "A lot of people don't like [to create] contingency plans because they take work, and you may never use them." We get it. There are so many things in your business that require your time and resources. Creating a plan for something that may never happen isn't high on your list of priorities.

You can't plan for everything. First, it's impossible to think of every scenario that may occur within your business. Second, there are not enough hours in your life to create a plan designed for each. So that's why we wrote this book.

Before we begin walking you through how to create a plan, you are going to focus on your business's foundation. You'll be tasked with understanding every detail of your business and then identifying potential crisis scenarios for which to plan. Then, we will walk you through the process of creating an effective yet flexible plan to respond to any scenario.

02 SWOT ANALYSIS

"Victory comes from finding opportunities in problems."
— Sun Tzu, Military Strategist

We're going to start off with some exercises that focus on getting to know your business. You're probably thinking, "What? I live and breathe my business! This is going to be a waste of my time." But bear with us. These will be what all of your plans are built off of, and the outputs may surprise you. The work you do in this chapter will be revisited later when building a plan, but some of this is information you should have on hand for reference.

WHAT IS A
SWOT

Many people may be familiar with Albert Humphrey's SWOT analysis, which identifies your **S**trengths, **W**eaknesses, **O**pportunities, and **T**hreats and organizes them into a two-by-two grid.

The value of performing a SWOT is in the information it provides you. This doesn't take a long time, and, once completed, you'll have a clear picture of not only *why* your customers choose to give you their money (Strengths) but also how you can grow or improve (Opportunities).

And you'll be forced to get honest with yourself on where your business is lacking (Weaknesses) and where you may be vulnerable either in the short or long term (Threats).

A SWOT analysis is a simple tool to help you not only understand your business but also strengthen your position.

How to perform a
SWOT ANALYSIS

A SWOT can be performed by yourself, with your leadership team, or even with your entire staff. There are no requirements for the number of participants, but more people bring a better perspective because you're more likely to be challenged on the items you list. More people mean more opinions and the potential for discussion. If, for example, you can't explain to or convince someone why something is a strength, maybe it isn't a strength. Don't be shy about asking for help with this important exercise. Your business will be better for it.

 Turn to **exercise one** in your workbook to complete a SWOT analysis, or draw a two-by-two grid on any blank piece of paper you have handy. This is a brainstorming activity where you are listing everything that comes to mind for each of the four categories. There are no wrong answers during the brainstorm.

In case you're having a hard time visualizing what we're talking about, we created an example SWOT for SpaceX.

SWOT ANALYSIS
SpaceX

STRENGTHS	WEAKNESSES
• Brand recognition • Innovative/first to market • Company culture • Intra-company collaboration	• Relevance • Technology may not be ready • Costly • Many unknowns/new industry
OPPORTUNITIES	THREATS
• Government contracts • Additional revenue streams • Provide more services to Earth	• Sources of funding dry up • May be ahead of time/dreaming too big • Intergalactic space pirates • Changes in political/cultural environment • Government competition/regulations

Spend 5 to 10 minutes in each category listing everything you and your team can.

Identify your
STRENGTHS

Think about the things that you do well. Do you have a strong team? Are your processes well defined? Do you have access to superior materials? Is your customer service the industry's gold standard?

Perform the exercise from different perspectives: What would your customers list as your strengths? What about your competition? Your vendors?

Know your strengths so that you know what it is that you should be planning to protect.

Identify your
WEAKNESSES

Listing out your business's weaknesses might feel unnatural, especially if you're in a position where everything seems to be going well. Be realistic. Consider every aspect of your business as you brainstorm this list. These should be internal (your employees, processes) and external (industry, suppliers, current political environment). What do your competitors do better than you? What's being held together with duct tape, either figuratively or literally?

Once you have looked at all the areas, brainstorm from the perspective of people outside your business. What would your customers or competitors list as weaknesses?

Know your weaknesses, so you can build a plan to bolster them. Knowing them will also help you avoid being blind-sided during an actual crisis.

Identify your
OPPORTUNITIES

It's time to flip back to a more positive view and look at opportunities that may exist within your business. Opportunities can be things like taking advantage of bulk discounts from vendors to expanding the footprint of your warehouse. This may even turn into a wish list of sorts.

Opportunities can be found in a new product or new service offerings. They can be about how, when, or where you sell. You can find opportunities with your employees, suppliers, and even your competition. Are there partnerships you could form with complementary businesses like a local brewery pairing its beers with a restaurant's menu items? That's similar to what one small business owner we know did.

During the writing of this book, we interviewed a restaurant owner in Charlotte, NC. His restaurant is very popular, especially on the weekends. If it's too busy inside, it's easy for the restaurant to send the customers who are waiting for a table next door to the brewery. After doing this for a few months, the restaurant realized they could sell takeout to those waiting customers in the brewery to increase their sales. Most businesses wouldn't want to drive business away like that, but with so many customers waiting for a table, an easy solution to reduce wait times is to sell your food to go.

But it was a pain for the restaurant to deal with either delivering the meals or coordinating with the customers on picking up their orders, so they made an offer to the brewery: The restaurant would supply the brewery with a point of sale station where they could enter in their own orders, and in return, the brewery would supply staff to take those orders, pick them up, and deliver to the customers in the brewery. The two businesses essentially merged their services in a scenario where everyone wins. The restaurant increases sales without having to increase staffing, the brewery keeps customers inside their building and provides them with a food service (which most breweries don't have, or they rely on food trucks). The customers get the best services and products the two businesses have to offer. Complete win-win-win for the restaurant, the brewery, and the customers!

Listing out your opportunities should be the fun part of the exercise, especially if you're doing this with your team because it allows you to think about all the great ways you can improve your business. You will likely identify some quick wins that you want to take advantage of. But, keep them on the drawing board. You have one more category to fill in.

Identify your
THREATS

Now back to the less fun stuff. Think about anything that could disrupt your business: key employees leaving, supply chain disruptions, heavy dependency on a single supplier, slow-pay customers, or even your competition rolling out a new product—anything that's a threat to how you do business today. These can be things that could happen without any notice or something that may take years before it affects your business. But, make sure it's timely. We spoke with a company in the aviation industry about the threats to their business. There's been a steady decline in the small, personal aircraft industry primarily because there are fewer new pilots and aircraft owners every year. This wasn't viewed as a threat to the business owners, though, because they would likely be retired before it had any real effect on their business. So, that is a threat, just not to them.

Look at threats from every angle you can think of. How do your customers view your business? Your employees? The competition? What threats exist for your location? Are there laws that are changing that may impact your business? What about your supply chain? Do you use materials that would be hard to obtain if your main supplier suddenly couldn't fulfill your orders?

The more threats you identify, the more secure you can make your business.

Prioritize and define
YOUR SWOT

Remember when we said there were no wrong answers? Well, you may have realized there were probably some wrong answers. Did you have some heated discussions about which category something belonged in? Is that one thing you listed as a strength potentially a weakness? Did you realize that your weaknesses may actually be opportunities? If so, that's okay. It's also possible for something to exist in more than one category.

We spoke with a dentist who is also a partner in a merchant services company who found out the hard way what his strengths and weaknesses were. Before the COVID-19 pandemic, he listed his sales strategy as a strength. His main customers were in the medical field and primarily dentists. That makes sense. He talks the same language as his customers, so it made it easy to sell his services. But, what happens when a pandemic closes the doors of 90% of your customers? Yep. You lose the vast majority of your income. So, that strength was quickly added to the weakness category when he realized he needed to diversify his customer base. If he had completed a SWOT analysis and defined his strengths, he may have been able to identify that his strength was also a weakness.

Now that you know why this is important, prioritize your strengths, weaknesses, opportunities, and threats based upon impact, timeliness, or anything that makes sense to you. Then, define the top five in each category. Write a sentence or two explaining them and why they belong in that category. For an idea of what we're referring to, check out the table below. You should be able to explain your reasoning to any random passerby who, for some reason, is interested in analyzing your SWOT. Those people exist, we swear! Okay, it may only be us, but can you convince your spouse why something is a strength?

 Complete **exercises two through five** in your workbook to prioritize and define your SWOT analysis.

Now that your SWOT exercise is complete, here is our prioritized explanation of the SWOT for SpaceX, including our definitions for each.

Note: We aren't SpaceX employees, and (sadly) we didn't get to sit down with Elon Musk to complete this SWOT, so our list is short. Your SWOT should have more than a handful in each category.

STRENGTHS
Definitions and Action Plans

Strength	Definition	Action Plan
Brand recognition	When someone says the name SpaceX or Elon Musk, what do people think of? Energy, innovation, the future. For people close to him or his industries, they are inspired. This helps recruit the best and brightest to invest in the company and to work for him.	• Continue to promote brand in unique ways • Encourage growth and innovation • Challenge team to stay on cutting edge
Innovation/first to market	SpaceX embodies the think and dream big personality that Elon Musk is known for. His companies and employees are an extension of that.	• Build strategic roadmap for growth • Encourage growth and innovation • Continue recruiting best and brightest
Intra-company collaboration	Elon Musk owns other companies such as Tesla that can be easily leveraged to create a synergy with SpaceX to help both improve upon future technology.	• Leverage resources between organizations • Provide growth opportunities for employees to move from company to company, incentive for top performers to stay within the Musk umbrella • Treat company roadmaps as confidential unless employees are covered by NDA for all companies
Company culture	The company culture attracts a skilled workforce because SpaceX is a desirable employer to work for.	• Continue to stay relevant and treat employees well • Keep it edgy and challenging

WEAKNESSES
Definitions and Action Plans

Weaknesses	Definition	Action Plan
Costly	New technology is rarely cheap, and testing new technology that has explosive material built into it is the opposite of inexpensive.	• Continue to innovate and collaborate—costs drop as technology is improved upon • Continue to market company to private investors
Technology may not be ready	SpaceX has improved their technology significantly over the past years, but there are still many kinks to work out. Being the new technology, while impressive, makes them less desirable right now than traditional planetary travel methods.	• Encourage innovation • Embrace failures as opportunities to learn • Continue to find additional uses for technology—offset costs by creating consumer products
Many unknowns/new industry	They are pioneers both physically and technologically in an arena that little is known about. There's a lot of theory going into their business, and it may not hold true.	• Create mitigation plans for potential problems • Keep open minds for solutions • Embrace failures as opportunities to learn
Relevance	Just like the country lost interest in space travel once we conquered the moon, SpaceX will need to constantly need to push the bar to stay relevant with current and potential investors.	• Create demand for the business through additional services such as planetary wifi • Stay on top of social media and marketing

OPPORTUNITIES
Definitions and Action Plans

Opportunities	Definition	Action Plan
Additional revenue streams	As the company grows, they improve upon their technology, and help lead us permanently into space, the options for exploiting that for profits will become readily available to them.	• Create a team dedicated to repurposing technology for other consumer products • Potential for partnerships to deliver value • Continue working on government contracts
Government contracts	From a economic and militaristic point of view, most world governments have their eyes on space as the next battleground both figuratively and literally. There will be a race to dominate and private companies like SpaceX will be heavily sought after.	• Utilize government contracts to stay on cutting edge • Position business in such a way that if they become "critical infrastructure" they still have control over their business
Provide more services to Earth	SpaceX is a company built on good will as well as innovation, and the opportunity to give more back to Earth such as satellite provided wifi will help drive their culture and keep them relevant.	• Planetary wifi • Space tourism • Partner with mining/drilling companies · interstellar taxi service

THREATS
Definitions and Action Plans

Threats	Definition	Action Plan
May be ahead of time/dreaming too big	They may be thinking and looking too far ahead to realize that they'll trip on something right below their feet.	• Keep it realistic - have both achievable and stretch goals • Embrace failures and encourage innovation
Government competition/regulations	Just like government contracts are opportunities, the governments themselves could regulate the company out of business.	• Brainstorm goals for future of the company—boutique space firm • Stay on top of laws and regulations and maintain relationships with lawmakers
Changes in political/cultural environment	Space exploration and exploitation are popular and accepted now both in government and with the public, but that could change at any moment based upon current events or just basic opinion.	• Remain flexible and be ready to pivot • Maintain social media and marketing to stay relevant • Maintain relationships with lawmakers
Sources of funding dry up	The company will always need to be working with current investors as well as looking for new investors to help fund their business. Without them, they will struggle to remain a leader in the industry.	• Stay relevant • Diversify investors • Diversify services offered
Intergalactic space pirates (ISPs)	It's only a matter of time that we attract the attention of ne'er-do-wells from another solar system as we expand into ours. We need to be prepared. While we don't anticipate ISPs any time soon, our point is that you need to think outside the box.	• Establish a lunar base • Invest in shield technology • Laser beams

Nice work on completing your first step to surviving a future disaster. We go more into the details on how to leverage your SWOT in **PART II: PLAN**.

What is your
SECRET SAUCE?

There's at least one reader out there who does, in fact, make and sell sauce. The rest of you should think figuratively. Your secret sauce is the thing that makes your business special. What is it that you do that no one else does better? Why do your customers continue to come back? Here are some examples of companies and their secret sauce to show you that it could be anything:

- **Amazon**—They can deliver ANYTHING in 2 days or less

- **Nordstrom**—Customer service

- **Apple**—Beautiful design and user-friendly products

- **Geico**—Marketing themselves

As you can see by the examples, your secret sauce can be anything, and it doesn't even have to be a secret. You just need to be better at it than anyone else.

Julie:

I once worked with a client in food distribution who had more independent (non-chain, non-franchise) restaurant business than any other food distributor within a five-state area. Because of the way that the distribution industry is set up, this meant higher margins for them. Additionally, their reputation was such that restaurant owners were calling them to schedule service versus their sales staff having to make cold calls to potential clients. Small businesses wanted to buy from them. Their secret sauce was quick delivery and exceptional customer service. The customers were clearly the priority for everyone in their company, from the forklift driver to the AP clerk. They were all trained to focus on delivering quality service, and they never had a shortage of prospects knocking on their door.

 Take a few minutes to brainstorm your secret sauce in **exercise six** in your workbook.

Did you discover something that you didn't know? Maybe you truly do have the world's best cup of coffee, but is that really why customers are coming through your doors every day? Or, is it because of your proximity to office buildings and you have a great training program for your staff? If the businesses in those office buildings all mysteriously closed one day, what would happen to your revenue? Dig deep when you're identifying your secret sauce.

Be honest with YOURSELF

Performing a SWOT isn't rocket science, but it can feel daunting, especially when you have to get honest about your weaknesses and threats. Don't fall victim to your ego. Take a hard look at every aspect of your business. If you don't like what the output of your SWOT says about your business, you don't have to show anyone, but you should start addressing the problems.

Every business has Strengths, Weaknesses, Opportunities, and Threats. The businesses that can sustain through the tough times are the ones that acknowledge all pieces of their SWOT. They are the ones who actively address the outputs from their analysis.

We're going to take what you did here and start to build plans to protect your Strengths from potential Weaknesses and Threats. (Sorry, Opportunities. This book isn't for you.)

Tips for SOLOPRENEURS

If you are one of the millions of solopreneurs, ask someone close to you and your business to review your SWOT, and provide any additional thoughts once you have completed it. A SWOT can be challenging because it requires you to think outside the box and be honest with yourself. Having someone to challenge you will provide a huge benefit.

03 ENVIRONMENTAL SCANNING

"No amount of sophistication is going to allay the fact that all of your knowledge is about the past and all your decisions are about the future."
— Ian Wilson, Former Executive at General Electric

Corey:

When I was in the senior year of my undergrad, I had to take a class on environmental scanning. It was the one class that everyone in my school dreaded taking. It was a challenge. I had to pull more than one all-nighter to complete the assigned projects on time, but I learned the most from this class. Early in the semester, the class was discussing current events that could affect the industry they were planning on entering into after graduation. This was 2003/2004, so America was in the thick of the war in the Middle East, and that war was on everyone's list. My professor stopped the discussion and asked us to name a time in history when America wasn't preparing for, recovering from, or participating in a war. No one could answer. Yes, we would need to keep that in mind for our decisions as managers or business owners, but America being involved in a war wasn't a revolutionary discovery. We needed to dig deeper to find the things that were fads now but could become trends. We needed to read in between the lines to discover the advantages that our competitors would otherwise miss.

What is **ENVIRONMENTAL SCANNING** and why it is **IMPORTANT**

Environmental Scanning is the art of systematically exploring and interpreting the external environment to better understand the nature of trends and their likely future impact on your organization. Environmental scans originated in a business context as a tool for retrieving and organizing data for decision making. That sounds fancy, right? Well, we aren't fancy. Simply put, environmental scanning is being aware of what's happening outside of your business so that you can make informed decisions as a result. It's all about being proactive. Entire books have been written on the subject, including the textbook Corey purchased for his senior year class. We will be giving a brief overview and suggest that you do some more digging if this is an area that interests you.

Environmental scanning isn't something you do once a year. It's an ongoing process. It's something that you should be performing daily, and you're very likely doing it informally or subconsciously on a regular basis.

How many times have you been watching the news and thought to yourself, "Hmmm...that may likely affect customer demand" or something similar? The manufacturer who produces copper fittings knows that a union strike at the ports will likely increase the cost of materials or create a delay in the supply chain. The news didn't have to say, "Hey, copper users, you may have issues coming your way" for that manufacturer to identify a potential issue. That's environmental scanning. Yes, that's an obvious example, but it's the 30,000-foot view.

Scanning helps you to prepare for threats or opportunities that have yet to affect your business.

How and when to
SCAN

Environmental Scanning should become part of your regular process. The same way you look at your financial information daily, you should be performing an environmental scan. Make sure you're looking at more than the obvious. What's happening in your industry? Are there any significant world, national, state, or local events happening that could impact your business? What will the rippling effects be to your business if a new technology is released?

We recognize that the first few times you do an environmental scan, you may question if you're doing it correctly. Are you reading the right newspapers and websites? Are you listening to the correct news outlets for information? Is your industry's trade magazine biased?

Chances are the answers are both "yes" and "no." You probably read the same newspaper or tune in to the same newscast every day. They conform to your political or personal views and tell you the information you want to hear. Regardless of the source, they should be reporting on the same thing, but they may be spun in a way to fit the voice/policy/agenda of that source. It's your job to read into what is being said for more information. It's also a good idea to get outside of your echo chamber and check out what the other sides are saying.

We're reminded of an episode of *The Daily Show* when Jon Stewart was still the host. He was making fun of how a particular news story was being spun by Fox News versus CNN. The headline was something like "The war in Iraq." The difference is that one of the networks had an exclamation point at the end, and the other had a question mark:

"The war in Iraq!"

"The war in Iraq?"

They are the exact same statement with very different meanings. Your job isn't to figure out which news site is accurately reporting; it's to figure out if there is a threat to or opportunity for your business based upon what's happening. You need to consider both statements because environmental scanning has no political affiliation. Also, it's possible that something that could affect your business is getting buried under other news or is being omitted completely for any reason. When major events occur, that's often the only thing you will see on any news source potentially for days on end. Having an arsenal of alternatives to gather information is critical.

It seems like you'll be spending hours upon hours performing environmental scanning, but these scans will quickly become second nature to you. Ideally, you'll perform scans daily. At the very least, you'll perform them weekly.

A quick overview of how to scan is to simply start by reading headlines and not just headlines that align with your political or societal views. Don't complete a scan from just the comfort of your own echo chamber. Ask yourself if there is anything that could hurt or help your business in that article. A landslide in India won't affect your business if you own a boutique gym, but it could potentially affect you if a raw material used in your manufacturing facility is sourced from India. So, you should be able to quickly scan the headlines to determine if there's anything worth investigating in an article.

Environmental Scanning may be a new term to you, but being aware of what is happening around you or your businesses isn't new.

What you're
SCANNING FOR

Common areas to perform environmental scanning are technology, customers, economy, competition, and the political landscape, but it depends on what has the most impact on your business. Understanding the events, fads, and trends in these areas can help you set your business up for success and allow you to get an edge on your competition. These could occur in a variety of areas, which is why it's important to scan a wide range of worldviews. You could start by scanning a broad area and then take the data from that area and interpret it into scenarios and/or options.

Once you have completed that, you decide if it's something you want to act on. You could create a strategic direction based on the information and then decide to implement a change. You may not always decide to act on the information, but even having the awareness can benefit you in business. It could help you shift your model or expand into a whole new area. You want to start looking for two different types of information: events and fads. Both of these can turn into opportunities or threats.

Events are the things that generally occur alone and separate from everything else. It's the landslide in India. Events can be quick in the grand scheme of things, like the landslide, or could take years to complete, like a war. They also tend to be a bit easier to spot and determine how your business will be affected.

There are those events that haven't occurred that may or may not be coming your way. They could be winter storms or legislation in a country where you source materials. You can literally see these things from miles away, but you have to determine how they may impact your business. That's the fun part of scanning.

On the other hand, fads are more widespread and include everything from the way people are eating to whatever the popular clothing is at the time. Think everything '80s. The '80s were full of upbeat, poppy songs. It was big hair, flashy clothes, and tons of makeup. The response to that was the grunge scene in the early '90s, which brought a more muted appearance. Knowing that tastes and styles change, how would you have positioned your business to exist in both of those markets assuming popular trends affect some portion of your business? How would you have known what was going to change and when?

If you are, say, an accountant, pretend you sell trendy clothing. At what point would you have known to shift from neon to flannel? Would it have been when Nirvana released "Bleach" or when they released "Nevermind"? When they made it on MTV, and grunge became more mainstream? Two years separate those albums; that's a long time that could have been used to prepare or plan for a shift in business.

The key to fads is determining if they will turn into trends. The difference between the two is longevity. Ask yourself if you could make money off of the fad now and if you could make money off it ten years from now. If you can't make money off the idea a decade from now, you're likely dealing with a fad. There's absolutely no reason why you shouldn't look to profit off of fads, but you shouldn't base your entire business on one unless you have reason to believe it will turn into a trend. In our '80s to '90s example, people purchasing and wearing clothing is a trend. What type they wear is a fad.

Why should you perform environmental scans? The answer is obvious: know what to expect in your business and industry and how you can react to changes in fads and trends. You'll have a greater understanding of what is happening with the economy and how that could impact your business. You'll be better positioned to take advantage of opportunities and mitigate risk from threats.

Corey:

In my scanning class, my group had been assigned Outback Steakhouse Incorporated. So, we had to become experts not only in the restaurant industry and their brands (Outback Steakhouse, Bonefish Grill, Carrabba's) but in food and diet trends. We identified low carb diets as a potential trend that should be addressed and folded into the business model which was easy considering steak was the main course for one of the brands we were "managing." We did our research, we scanned the diet environment, and we determined that low carb was going to stick around for a while. Our instructor said we were wrong and that we should be focusing on home meal replacements instead. Yes, home meal replacements are still a thing, but when was the last time you bought a package of TGIF's frozen loaded potato skins from the store versus the last time you purchased a 12-pack of spiked seltzer? Considering that the low carb alcohol market alone was around $166 billion (that's billion, with a "B") globally in 2018, I would say that the low carb trend has been proven since 2003. (You hear that, Stu?)

Would it have been smart to change Outback's business model completely in 2003 to focus on those people with low carb, ketogenic, or even paleo diets? No. Would it have been smart for them to research and slowly introduce it into their model? Yes. Could they have been a leader in the low carb diet industry and made a ton of money off of it? Absolutely!

Where to
SCAN

Today, there are so many resources to use to perform your scans; you will have to pick a few that serve you best. Read the news when you're eating breakfast and listen to a podcast on your way to work. Social media has become the quickest way to find out what's going on in the world, so stay connected. Information is overly abundant and often cheap or free, so there's no reason why you shouldn't be informed. But only you will know what information is relevant to your business and industry and which sources will be of the most value.

Document
YOUR SCANS

Capturing the information from an environmental scan is simple. We found the easiest approach is to have a notebook dedicated to regular scans (daily or weekly, depending on your preference) and tracking each scan in the notebook. You can group your findings based on the type (technology, customers, weather, political, etc.) with a page or section noted for each. Keeping the data for each scan segregated makes it easier to spot trends within the respective types. But, this is a matter of preference. Find an approach that makes it easy to capture and review, and you're all set.

 Open your workbook to **exercise seven**, and get ready to do some scanning.

Awareness of COMPETITION

Environmental scanning raises the level of awareness you have for competition in your industry. You're probably well aware of what your direct competitors are doing, but what is someone doing on the other side of the globe? Your bicycle repair business may never compete directly against one in Germany, but that German repair shop may be using some cutting-edge technology that has yet to make it to where you live. While you may only have a local market, you will be researching and getting to know your industry outside of your market. Where are the trends set for your industry? Are you a restaurant owner in the Midwest? Should you be looking to food trends on the coasts knowing that they'll eventually make it to your city?

Environmental scanning will help you identify whatever is coming your way and give you time to plan for it.

04 PROCESS ANALYSIS

"Spend time upfront to invest in systems and processes to make long-term growth sustainable." — Jeff Platt, CEO of Sky Zone

ook, we admit going into this that this isn't going to be the sexiest chapter in the book. Talking about day-to-day functions like processes, financial information, and vendors are not exactly the stuff that gets your heart rate up (though it may increase your blood pressure), but it is critical. And we are going to do our very best to keep it interesting. It's like working your core at the gym: you may prefer to work on a part of your body that gets the most attention (like your abs), but you have to round it out. It's unlikely anyone has said "sweet lumbars" to you at the gym, so you're less likely to focus on strengthening those versus toning your biceps. But, you must work those back muscles to stay fit and strong. Welcome to process. Throw on a sweatband and get ready to work your brain.

Processes and procedures
DOCUMENTED

Let's start with the basics. What are processes and procedures?

- **Process**—a high-level operation that can span a department or the entire organization; how you define the steps needed to achieve the objective.

- **Procedure**—the specific protocol needed to accomplish part of the process.

Okay, let's clarify that with some examples. We are going to use something extremely common today: Posting to social media.

As an example, a post to Instagram would require a photographer to take a picture, a copywriter to write the text for the post, and perhaps a marketing resource to complete the posting. Each task within the overall process is listed. In your small business, one person may be completing all of these tasks, but you get the idea.

The procedure provides step-by-step instructions for completing the task. This would include how to log into Instagram, what the username and password are, where to navigate once inside the application, what to click to post, and even how to copy and paste the text to be included with the photo.

Not clear enough? How about this: Have you ever participated in one of those ice breakers or team building events where you have to write detailed instructions for something that shouldn't require instructions, like how to make a PB&J? You write out the instructions and give them to someone else to complete, and they aren't allowed to deviate from the instructions at all. It's simple! You get some bread, put some peanut butter on one piece, jelly on the other, and then slap them together. Bam! PB&J. Wrong. We aren't going to list it all out (because it will probably be wrong), but there are all sorts of steps like "get a knife" and "unscrew the lid" that need to be included in the procedure. There are certain details in processes that we take for granted because they're "common sense." But as we all know, not everyone has the same level of common sense. Think about that when you're reading this chapter as you may need to be more detailed than you expected.

That's a pretty high-level overview of processes and procedures. As you can see, they are related, but they are very different. To simplify even further:

Process = what you're doing

Procedure = how you do it

Importance of
PROCESS

Processes are important because they tell us what is happening in the business and allow us to review for improvement. They tell you exactly how your business should function and allow you to find areas where there may be deviations (for better or worse). To help you identify what processes are the most important, you're going to make a list of all the processes you can think of in your organization. But before you start, we want to give you some additional details to help you complete this successfully.

First, there's a sweet spot between too detailed and too vague that you'll have to find to make this useful. That sweet spot is where you can easily explain what it is that you're doing without getting bogged down in the details. In the PB&J example, the process would be "Make a PB&J." It's safe to assume that there would be no training required for this, but you may have some notes for whoever is making your lunch, such as putting peanut butter on both sides so the jelly doesn't make the bread soggy. If you were to task pretty much any adult with making you that PB&J, you'd probably get the PB&J you want. So, "Make a PB&J" is the process. "Remove lids," "use a knife to scoop out 2 Tbsp of peanut butter," etc. are the procedures.

Second, it may be easier to think of the big picture first and then divide that up into more bite-sized pieces. Start by thinking about the value chains in your business. Value chains are basically the high-level process used to describe how you perform something start to finish in your business and generally spans across more than one department. Even though you may think you have an ongoing process with no actual end, like marketing to customers, in reality, you are just cycling through the same series of processes in the larger value chain. You can name your value chains anything, but there are a few that are widely used in most industries. An example is "Procure to Pay." This will detail how you order, receive, and then pay for materials in your business. If you were in manufacturing, it could include:

- **Vetting and sourcing vendors**—Who is responsible for this? What decisions do they have to make? Is there an approval process? Who else is involved?

- **Vetting and sourcing materials**—What information is needed for the materials? Product costs? Lead time? Ordering multiples?

- **Onboarding a vendor**—Do they have to be entered into multiple systems? What information is needed from the vendor? Do you require a tour of their facility first?

You can see that this can be extensive, and you probably think you have more important things to do than to document your entire business. Well, it is extensive, and you do have more important things to do. We're going to make this as efficient as possible. You aren't going to be graded on this, so it's okay if you don't get it right the first time or if it doesn't match what a pro would build out for you. It needs to work for you.

 Turn to **exercise eight** in your workbook to begin your process exercises.

- First, list your value chains. What are those sweeping things happening across your business? It's fine if you don't have professional-sounding words for your value chains. You only need to identify them. That could be how your accounting department performs the financial side of the business or how your marketing person markets your business from start to finish.

- Second, list the main processes under each. Mentally walk through the whole process, noting those smaller buckets where things happen. Consider such tasks as onboarding or marketing to a customer, or performing inventory management (counting, rotating, etc.). Brainstorm as many as you can think of, even of those you aren't sure are important. Who cleans up the warehouse at the end of the day? There's a process involved that should be noted.

What are your
CRITICAL PROCESSES?

Now that you have done a short brainstorming session of all the processes you can think of, it's time to identify the processes that are the most important to your business. Your most critical processes are the ones that your business MUST execute for you to keep the doors open. It's time to walk through some examples.

- **Example 1**—You own a t-shirt printing shop. Your procurement process and your sales process are critical. You need both the materials to print on and someone to buy the printed shirts.

- **Example 2**—You run a very popular sandwich shop. Your sales and customer service processes are critical to your business.

- **Example 3**—You receive and process vendor invoices... Wait! That doesn't sound important. You don't make any money off of that, and in fact, you are paying money instead. But, what happens if you stop paying your vendors? Nearly everyone initially thinks of only those processes involved with generating revenue, so we wanted to make sure you were looking at the broad picture.

Knowing which processes are most important will be critical if you ever find yourself in a situation where your business has had to shut down temporarily for any reason. These processes are likely the ones you'll want to address first. You can review now for potential improvements because you may be able to make or save some time or money if they're running more efficiently.

 Turn to **exercise nine** in the workbook to list out all of your critical processes.

Document
PROCESSES

Processes are the backbone of your operation, whether they are currently documented or not. Therefore, having them written down (even at a high level) is going to benefit you and your business. This is true for several reasons.

First, it's easier to spot areas that need improvement if you observe close enough to document them; walk through these processes with your team to understand how the work is performed. There's a good chance what you think should be happening isn't actually happening. That could be for various reasons, but your team may have found a more efficient way to complete their work. You may also get complaints and suggestions about the processes, which are opportunities for improvement; you should be writing these down.

Second, what about that proverbial someone "gets hit by a bus" scenario? We suppose "wins the lottery" is more appropriate nowadays because it sounds friendlier. Regardless, your GM is a no-show for work today, and no one knows why. Who can do their job? What is their job? What have they quietly or silently been struggling to hold together? Something no one else knew about until now? Having your processes documented allows you to see bottlenecks or areas where you're spread thin.

Third, a well-documented process makes virtually everyone in the company replaceable. Yes, even you. This is a good thing. Now you know where you may need help if your business expands. You also know where you can cut if it contracts. You may even now know who to hire to take things off of your plate so that you can focus on building your business or simply improving your backswing. It gives you knowledge about your business.

Turn to **exercise ten** in your workbook to begin documenting one process. We will start by breaking this down into bite-sized pieces. The four simple steps to documenting a process are:

- **Step 1**—Ask high-level questions about the process in general and not about what is being done.

  - Is it necessary?
  - Is it efficient?

- Is it relevant?

- Is it logical?

While this may seem odd, you first want to confirm that a process is being performed —no sense in documenting something you no longer do. We aren't documenting for the sake of documenting. We want to be as efficient with your time as possible.

- **Step 2**—Write the process down and assign a single owner to each step. Processes will likely span across many roles, so you at least have the departments correct. If, for example, you're documenting the AP process, you don't have to put "Aaron in accounting" as the task owner. You could, but what if Aaron wins the lottery (or, you know, gets hit by a bus)? You'll have to update. Instead, "Accounting" or the role title is fine. If it's a large process, you may want to approach it in smaller pieces. Some folks like to draw the process; others like to use a bulleted list. It doesn't matter. It's all personal preference, so find what works and start writing.

Here's a quick process for receiving and paying an invoice:

It's very simple, and it's missing a lot. But, you see what is being performed and by whom. Write down these processes and let your team review them. This was made in PowerPoint. You can use a process tool like Visio or Lucidcharts. You can draw even them on a whiteboard (just remember to take a picture when you're finished).

- **Step 3**—Test the process. Have someone run through the process using exactly what you have documented. It's time to see if they can make you that PB&J. This helps not only confirm if the steps are correct but also that they can be followed by someone other than the author. An important time for a side note here—unless you're the only person in your company, you don't necessarily have to be the person documenting the processes. Assign this to people on your team. Share the fun.

- **Step 4**—Review with your team. Now that the process has been tested, review the process with the entire team. This review is going to help you determine what needs to be improved or incorporated into the plan. We will review this piece in more detail later.

Helpful **TIPS:**

- Put the processes someplace they are easy to find. If you completed this on paper, make some extra copies so you can use them for training new hires. Wait—new hires? Yup, you created training materials for your business. If you created this electronically, have a filing system on your computer that makes them easy to find.

- Don't "set it and forget it." Review the processes to confirm they're still relevant, to look for opportunities to gain efficiencies, and to confirm that the processes still work. These reviews should occur when there are changes in your business, such as changes in personnel or improvements in technology or the business model.

- There are hundreds and probably thousands of books that you can reference for more on documenting, reviewing, and improving processes. A couple of quick reads, if you're interested: *The Ultimate Guide to Business Process Management: Everything You Need to Know and How to Apply It to Your Organization* by Theodore Panagacos and *Value-Driven Business Process*

Management: The Value-Switch for Long Lasting Competitive Advantage by Peter Franz and Mathias Kirchmer. (The book titles may actually be longer than the books themselves.)

That was a somewhat brief overview of process analysis for your business. It's a lot of work, but the results will pay for themselves. Nice job, and oh...sweet lumbars, bro.

Tips for
SOLOPRENEURS

When it comes to processes as a solopreneur, you may outsource more work than a business with employees. So make sure you pay attention to areas where an external resource (like an accountant) completes a step in the process. You may not know all of the steps they perform, but you should be confident in the output that you receive back from them. It is also a good idea to identify backups for those roles as you have no control over availability or capacity.

05 BUSINESS OPERATIONS

"Far and away the best prize that life offers is the chance to work hard at work worth doing."
— Theodore Roosevelt, 26th President of the United States

FINANCIALS

Overview

Did you start to squirm when you read "Financials"? For whatever reason, this is an area in which a lot of small business owners struggle. No judgment because unless you own and run an accounting firm, an accounting background is not required to open and operate a small business. We're going to briefly touch on some basic concepts and then cover what you really need to know for crisis planning.

First, you should have an accountant you trust. There are so many services they can provide if they're good at what they do—everything from the basic tax prep to financial advice. We can't stress enough how important it is to pay an accountant to do the work you likely aren't an expert at. Now, there's nothing better than an accountant who knows you and your business, but being able to keep an eye on them is smart, so we recommend that you learn a little to "keep them honest." This isn't a finance course, so it's up to you to determine what your level of knowledge should be.

The
BASICS

As you think about your company's financials, it's not uncommon to head straight to your profit and loss statements (P&L) or to think about sales targets, year over year growth, and even specific monthly expenses. Those are important numbers to have in mind, but there are other areas of finance that we want you to keep in mind as you're working through a plan.

Having a list of important information is extremely helpful in stressful situations. If you have things like your bank account numbers, bank contact phone numbers, etc. written down in one spot, it will make contacting the people that much easier. Keep in mind that someone else may be making these calls if you happen to be stranded in another country trying to make your way back home from vacation in order to respond to an emergency.

It's also a good idea to put someone you trust on your bank account in case there's an emergency and you're unavailable. This doesn't even have to be an employee. It could be your best friend from college who lives down the street. Have the information and a way for someone to access it. That way, when you hit your head and get amnesia like Fred Flintstone, someone can still access the bank. (See, we told you there would be a cartoon reference in here.)

Cash is king, and cash flows keep your business afloat. With that in mind, it is helpful to have a good rapport with your bank and to have credit lines set up just in case. Being able to quickly and easily tap into a credit line or execute a loan will speed up the process of recovery. We all know how slowly banks can move, so put in place what you can now.

Sample
NUMBERS, RATIOS, ETC.

Most business owners only care to know how to read their monthly/annual profit and loss statement, also known as your income statement. That makes sense because it states what you made or lost. But, some would argue that the statement of cash flows is the most important because it indicates where you are getting and using cash and how much you have. (Everyone agrees the balance sheet is worthless...Maybe it's only Corey). You should get to know both in detail because they both provide great information, and you should definitely be reviewing these monthly. If you aren't financially minded, spend some time with your accountant or someone in that area who can walk you through everything. Don't be embarrassed if you aren't financially knowledgeable. You are great at what you do and can pay someone else to be great at what they do.

We can sit here and tell you all the reasons you want to know your current ratio or debt to equity ratio (which, ironically enough, come from the balance sheet). Yes, you should be able to figure these out and track them as they do provide you with the overall financial health of your business. But what do they mean? Well, everything and nothing. It depends so much on your business and industry that there's no way to generalize what they should be and what that means to you. If you recently took on a new loan for a large piece of equipment, your numbers may be off compared to your competitors. You should be able to explain it if someone asks, and the only time they may ask is when you're looking for money from them either as a loan or when you're selling your business. No one will care about most of these on a regular basis.

You should get to know your industry and benchmark yourself against your competitors. You will likely only be able to find information on publicly traded companies as well as generalized numbers for your industry, but that's enough to get you going. Every industry is different, but that information is out there. You may need to do some legwork to find them. We couldn't even begin to suggest where to look because it varies so much. Start with the Internet?

There are numbers that you should know and track monthly because they're all about cash flow. The better your cash flow, the better prepared you are to respond to a crisis. Those numbers are days payable, days receivable, and days inventory on hand.

Days payable is a measure of how long it takes you to pay an invoice once received. Generally speaking, the larger the number, the better. That means you're holding onto your money as long as possible.

Days receivable is a measure of how long it takes your customers to pay you. The smaller the number, the better. That means your customers are paying you quickly. If you are in a transactional business like a restaurant or online retail, your days receivable should be zero, as people pay at the time of service. That's great!

Days inventory on hand (DIO) is a measure of how large your inventory is, which affects cash flow. Money tied up in inventory is money you can't use elsewhere. Your goal for this is to make it as efficient as possible, which can be high, low, or anywhere in between. It's what makes sense for your business. A restaurant with a high DIO will likely have some spoilage issues since some food doesn't hold that long. An auto parts store could have a large DIO because most parts won't ever "go bad," so it doesn't matter as much. Figure out what it costs you to order, receive, and hold that inventory and how quickly you can turn it over.

You'll also need to consider how you're ordering. Can you order in bulk to get a discount? If so, is that worth it if it's going to take you twice as long to sell through it? There are formulas out there to calculate the most efficient way to order. It's worth looking into and would be an entire book by itself. Bottom line: The closer you can get your DIO to the most efficient amount, the more cash you're going to have in your pocket.

You may be saying to yourself right now that you don't carry inventory, you sell a service. You're a graphic designer or a lawyer or a therapist. No worries. You can calculate another element of your business. How long does it take to complete a job? What costs go into it? What's your average customer invoice for each job? Whereas an inventory-heavy business will be calculating how quickly they can turn their inventory, you'll be calculating how quickly you can turn your resources.

Financial
GOALS

Finally, you should create a set of financial goals for your business, primarily as a safety net. Everyone has a different comfort level with financial risk, so determine what's comfortable for you. We recommend that you set aside (or create a goal to have) a certain amount of cash on hand at all times. This should be calculated as a percentage of your average monthly expenses. So, say it costs $10,000/month to run your business (all in) and you want to have 3 months of expenses on hand, that's $30,000 you should have in your bank accounts or something very liquid—inventory shouldn't be considered in this as you may not be able to sell when a crisis hits. Other goals you should set could be a certain debt percentage for the company or even your own personal credit score. The stronger you make yourself financially, the better off you will be during hard times.

Phew! That's it on financials. We could go into depth about plenty of other areas, but the main takeaways are that you and those you trust can access your bank account and lines of credit and that you're maximizing your cash flow.

The more liquid you are, the more prepared you are.

PROFESSIONAL SERVICES

Defining professional
SERVICES

For the purposes of this book, we're going to include Insurance, Legal, Marketing, Accountants, Financial Advisors, and IT Consultants as part of this category. We understand that each of these areas could be a chapter (or entire book!), but we are only looking at these services from the perspective of how to plan and respond to a crisis.

INSURANCE

The single most important thing we want to emphasize for insurance is this: understand your coverage! Look no further than COVID-19 to find the reason why. Many people didn't realize that as a direct result of the SARS outbreak in 2003, insurance carriers changed their business interruption insurance to no longer cover pandemics. Most small business owners didn't realize this change occurred and expected their carrier to pay out. Surprise! (Honestly, we can't think of a worse surprise.)

Review your policies, and get your agent to help you understand your coverage. Most policies renew annually, so you have an opportunity once every 12 months to review your coverages. It's important to understand what's covered and how your carrier will pay. From a crisis perspective, you'll likely have a task in your plan that reads *contact insurance agent* (if the crisis is significant and results in physical or financial damage).

Don't put yourself in a position where you are surprised and it's too late to make a change.

LEGAL

Many small businesses don't need a full-time attorney on staff, and there are plenty of small businesses that have never used an attorney. If you've never used one, we are going to recommend that you at least build a relationship with an attorney now so that you have someone to leverage in the event of a crisis. And it's 100% okay to say, "Hey, I don't need an attorney now, but I'm doing crisis planning, and I want to establish a relationship should I need someone in the future." That's smart planning.

Ask your trusted advisors who they use as an attorney for their small business needs and then ask for an introduction. Repeat until you find someone you feel comfortable with and then build the relationship. Keep the information handy and add a task to the crisis plan to *contact my attorney, if needed*. You're all set.

MARKETING

If you're a small business owner who outsources your marketing, consider how that is impacted in a crisis. If the crisis is limited to only your business or a very small number of businesses (maybe a fire swept through the block your business is located on), then you'll want to handle that differently than if it's a global pandemic. Understanding what your marketing calendar looks like is key, especially when you must decide to pause all communications quickly. When a marketing calendar is planned in advance, a fire, hurricane, or any other crisis isn't considered. The last thing you want to do is send messaging to your customers that is confusing or worse yet, tone-deaf.

Have a conversation with your marketing expert while you're doing crisis planning. He or she may have valuable insight to help you create the tasks around marketing in your plans.

Accountants and financial
ADVISORS

Don't worry. We aren't going to ask you to math again. We might be tough, but we aren't mean.

Because we already covered finance, the only thing we will say about accountants is that when a crisis happens, you'll want to have a conversation with your accountant early on in the process, so you're both on the same page. If you don't have an accountant, get one or at least create a relationship with one.

Your accountant and financial advisor may be one and the same, but in the event they aren't, we need to address this professional service as well. Because your financial advisor is focused on helping you meet your financial goals, you'll need to work with him or her at some point during a crisis. It's probably not your first call, but once things settle down and your business is beginning to normalize, have a conversation with your financial advisor.

Talk to your financial advisor while you're doing crisis planning. He or she may have valuable input to the plan.

IT
CONSULTANTS

Raise your hand if you have an outside resource (consultant) managing technology for your small business. If technology isn't a core strength for you, then hiring someone to manage that work is a smart move for your business. We're big believers in focusing on your strengths and paying someone else to do the things not in your wheelhouse when you can afford to do so. In the case of IT consultants, your first step is understanding the agreement in place. In some instances, this may be an annual contract where the consultant is responsible for all regular work. In other instances, it could be an arrangement where the consultant only performs work when you make a request.

Regardless of the arrangement, review the agreement in place and talk to an IT consultant about crisis planning, especially if all of your work is outsourced. Understand how your IT consultant will work with you during a crisis and what you can expect in terms of response times.

They can also help you set up backup systems just in case your on sight technology washes away with the flood waters. Even better: third party vendors generally have an off site solution that you can access remotely. Keep in mind where they're located, though, because if they get hit with the disaster, you may be out of luck.

VENDORS

Basic vendor MANAGEMENT

You should view your vendor relationships as business partnerships. Your vendors provide you a service or a product for your hard-earned cash, but they can also provide information—and potentially resources—throughout the course of business and if times get tough. At a minimum, you should have your vendors' contact information available for anyone who may need it, much like you would with your financial and other contact info. You may not always be around to make the call. You should also include back up vendor information when possible in case your primary supplier is the one dealing with the warehouse fire.

Corey and Julie:

We worked for a food distributor who had a customer with a handful of stores in the region, and the distributor had 100% of the customer's business. It was good money and an easy customer to work with until there was a procurement SNAFU. The customer sold whole rotisserie chickens, and the distributor ran out. Well, they were lucky that they only lost one of the accounts. The customer switched over one store to a competing distributor so that they could have access to that vendor's inventory without having to worry about whether or not our client could supply what they needed. After that, our client was competing harder than ever to make sure they didn't lose the rest of the business. They screwed up and paid for it by allowing their competitor into their customer's business. The customer learned a valuable lesson that they shouldn't have their entire business dependent upon one vendor to supply them.

Active vendor management allows your company to control costs better, reduce the possibility of disruption in service, and optimize performance. Vendor management provides your organization with better selection, stronger contract management, and better value. That doesn't mean you should threaten to leave or switch vendors regularly. We have had clients who had customers who did that and let's just say those customers weren't treated well by any of their vendors.

Your best bet with your vendors is always to be looking for a win-win solution. They are in the business to make money. So are you. So, while it's okay to look for lower prices from your vendors, you shouldn't expect to negotiate every time, or you'll soon realize that you aren't a very good customer. Calculate everything into the cost of doing business, not only the cost of the product. You may be paying more for your products, but there may be a good reason for that. Win-win.

CONTRACTS

Vendors are so closely tied to the success of your business, yet it's a component that many business owners give little thought to. Find a supplier who can meet your needs at a decent price and move forward.

If only it were that simple...

Most companies deal with numerous vendors (it's not uncommon for medium to large-sized businesses to work with hundreds of vendors), and when you're counting on a third party to deliver goods or services, you want to make sure you have a good relationship AND a good contract.

Whether you're working on a new vendor contract or negotiating a current contract, be sure you can work everything in your favor, from regulations to order accuracy. Even if you can't get a guarantee on order accuracy, you may be able to work out some side deals with your sales rep if you can prove that the vendor hasn't been holding up their end of the bargain. You want to know how these situations will be handled before they occur, and the best way to do that is to have it included in the contract.

More than likely, you won't be big enough or have enough influence to get all favorable terms regarding payment or order accuracy, but make sure you're covered should they have some sort of issue on their end with their product. You want to be able to pass the buck if they sold you something defective that you passed along to your customers. The last thing you want is a lawsuit against you because you didn't do your due diligence in vetting your vendor.

So what was this chapter all about? It's so that you can organize your external services in a way that makes it easy to reference. Before we move on to the next section, we provided a space in the workbook in **exercise eleven** for you to list out all the names and numbers you could think of as well as contact information.

EXIT STRATEGIES

Options for
YOUR BUSINESS

Before we move on to the next chapter, we want to take a minute to talk about the option of exiting your business. People go into business for many reasons, and thankfully the world is full of supportive people, classes, books, podcasts, etc. on how to start your own business.

What seems to be in short supply is the information on when and how to exit your business.

Now, we love small businesses and hate to see anyone close down, but the reality is businesses close every day, and we would prefer your business close because you chose to shut the doors rather than it being forced on you. If you're considering an exit strategy, here are the most common options available to business owners:

- **Shut down**—You decide to go out of business. You build an intentional plan for shutting down your business and announce it to your customers.

- **Keep business in the family**—In this instance, you step away from the business but keep it in the family. Maybe you even stay on in some capacity, but you are no longer managing the day to day operations.

- **Sell to a competitor**—You become an acquisition for a competitor. This is the exit strategy people are most familiar with, but it's not the most common for small businesses. In this instance, you're marketing your business to a particular competitor with whom you are familiar.

- **Sell the business to managers/employees**—This approach is generally very successful for small business owners as you are selling to someone who already knows what you do and is probably already helping you run the business anyway.

- **Sell on the open market**—Similar to selling to a competitor only you don't have a target company in mind to purchase your business. You're announcing that your business is for sale and then seeing what offers come your way.

Exit
CONDITIONS

As you can see, exiting can be approached in a variety of ways. The question you should be asking yourself is: Under what conditions would I exit?

Turn to **exercise twelve** in the workbook and start listing out the triggers for you personally. There's this saying "everyone has a price," and we have found that to be true. If there's a good enough offer put on the table, would you say yes?

Here are some possible triggers to consider:

- An offer you can't refuse

- Ready for retirement

- Hit your financial goals, and it's time to let your kids (or sibling, etc.) take over

- Global financial crisis and you can't stay afloat

- Business is no longer relevant (example: you own a typewriter repair business)

- You realize you hate your business

- You realize you aren't cut out to run a business

Having a list of triggers identifying when and if you would exit is a great exercise to go through.

Corey and Julie:

> We had a client who received an offer from a competitor to buy his small business. Our client was angry that the offer was made. He viewed that offer as an indictment on his ability to run his business. It actually fueled him to push harder, deliver more value to his customers, and to put some systems and processes in place that didn't exist prior to the offer. By the time our client contacted us to tell us about the offer, he already had his mind made up. He knew he didn't want to sell because we had worked with him months prior on defining the triggers in which he would exit his business.

If you receive an offer that's too good to pass up, you'll know it when you see it. But if you never gave thought to under what conditions you would exit, and now you're staring down the barrel of an offer, you may have to act quickly. You don't want to end up in a situation where you regret the choice you made. Have a plan. Spend a few hours now giving it thought so that it's easier down the road.

06 GAP ANALYSIS

"Most people spend more time and energy going around problems than in trying to solve them."
— Henry Ford, Business Magnate

Julie:

I once ran the engineering department for a small software company, and the CEO asked me to run a special project for him. He had a product that was not selling as well in the market as was forecasted, and he wanted the problem fixed. He wanted this particular product to be his #1 seller. So, he gave me a ridiculous budget and said, "Spend this however you want but fix the product. You have 90 days."

Never had I approached a project with such enthusiasm. I was leading it. I owned all of the decisions and all of the outcomes. Nobody was standing in my way. I could take any team members I wanted and put them on my team. I took all of the best people, and I built a veritable dream team to solve the product issues. In less than 90 days, we were able to do a complete turn-around on the product. We fixed issues; we added features; we built a road map for the next 18 months. The team was on fire.

But as one product climbed in sales, the other products within the organization plummeted. Scheduled releases of new features and bug fixes fell behind schedule or didn't happen at all. Promises made to existing and new customers weren't met. Why?

I was so focused on my project that I wasn't thinking about the other products that existed within the company. There was a huge gap in my plan: my plan only included one priority. I was singularly focused on achieving one goal.

That focus left a significant void within the company. I had taken all of the best resources. I fixed issues in one product without thinking about the consequences of our remaining products. I unintentionally created gaps for every other team.

What is a
GAP

Gaps in this respect are areas where something is lacking. They could be (but aren't necessarily) gaping holes in your processes. More likely, your processes still occur, but maybe there's something that can be improved upon. Gaps can be risks of which you weren't aware or opportunities for improvement. It's now time to find your gaps.

Tools to
IDENTIFY GAPS

You probably already have an idea of areas where you can improve your business. They could be little annoyances or larger flaws, but you live with them. The gaps you are unaware of are generally discovered during the process review. These could be things that are missing completely or simply a task that someone is performing to fill in the gap. While it may be good to know that someone on your team is putting in the extra work to keep your business running, it's a problem because it's not documented or known and can't be measured or tracked.

To perform your gap analysis, review your processes. Then, pick one process from your list that you think is critical, and walk through it from start to finish. Ideally, you'll perform this walk through with everyone who is involved in the process to get their input. Now, it doesn't *have* to be *everyone*. If you have multiple sales managers and are doing a sales process, pick one manager to represent the group.

It's great if you can get everyone into a conference room together, but you don't need to pull everyone away from their jobs at the same time. You could perform these individually with each role while they're performing that task in the process. You could pull everyone together after hours or during downtime for 30 minutes a day. You can do this however works best for your schedule. The important part is that you're reviewing your processes.

As for materials, it will be a better use of your team's time if you have a copy of the process for them to review ahead of time. It's also helpful to have the entire process from start to finish so that everyone can visualize what occurs and spot errors or opportunities. It allows them to understand what happens up and downstream from them. So, a giant print-out, a PowerPoint presentation, a bunch of hand-drawn processes on giant sticky notes—whatever works for you.

We also recognize that walking through processes is time-consuming, so feel free to spread the work out over several weeks or months. When we were reviewing a value chain for a previous client, we set up a schedule of one hour a week over about three months to meet with their team. This approach didn't affect their weekly responsibilities because it was such a small ask of their time. Pick the slowest afternoon (or evening) of the week and leverage a few hours to walk through your processes. Your customers and business will thank you for it.

Find the
GAPS

Now that you have your processes documented, you can begin looking for ways to improve upon your business. This is another brainstorming session with the group that helped you document the original process. You can likely improve some way you do business, and it's possible that maybe you documented something incorrectly.

If you aren't receiving feedback during this review, ask questions around how it affects each department, if there are any issues with the timeliness of this step, or what could be done to speed up the process. Make sure you're documenting (or having someone document) everything that's being said. This will be used to create the desired future state of your business.

If you want to get even more feedback on the processes, you can then open it up to the whole team to review. This could be done by sharing electronically or posting the paper processes on a wall in the office for everyone to review. Put some markers or sticky notes nearby and allow everyone to see what they do and make their own comments. It can be anonymous, but having them include their name makes it easier to follow up if you have questions.

You may get conflicting comments, so you'll have to compromise or tell someone "tough luck," but usually you'll get constructive feedback. Everybody wants their job to be easier, right?

So, what is the point of all of this regarding preparation for a crisis? First, it helps you know where you may be lacking so that it is not a surprise. Your Internet going down could be a crisis, but you identified that as a gap during your process review allowing you to create a back-up solution. Second, it will hopefully allow you to strengthen those areas that may be weak so that they're less likely to break under stress. We're building a better, stronger business now so that it can withstand a storm later.

Return on Investment and
BUSINESS CASES

 Open up your workbooks and turn to **exercise thirteen** to begin the gap analysis process.

List everything that you identified as improvement opportunities or risks during your process review. Some of these may have been easy that were fixed during the process review. For example, accounting couldn't identify who was approving invoices so you now have managers signing their name on the physical copy. Easy. Others may take some time and training and others may include some sort of financial investment. List them all out.

Start with a "nice to have" versus "need to have" approach to grouping them. Sure, it would be nice to automate the internal procurement process, but the process works fine as-is, and that would cost money that you don't want to spend. On the other hand, the reason your production process has a bottleneck is that a particular vendor has fulfillment issues, and it's time to find another vendor.

Once you have made your two groups, you'll want to factor a few things into your decision. The goal of this is to calculate a return on investment (ROI) for any gap that you're addressing (or any project in general) and then potentially create a business case. We highly recommend you perform these at a very high level at least to ensure the work and investment you're about to make is worth it.

- **Cost—**What will this cost both in time and cash? This could be anything from the negative effect of pulling away resources to use elsewhere, the cash you have to spend to complete the project, or the additional ongoing costs of expanding your business, such as additional payroll.

- **Return—**What will you stand to gain if you fill the gap? This can range from revenue gains to employee well-being. In simple terms: it's any positive effect on your business.

You now have everything needed to perform a quick ROI for each. We do mean quick— especially for those things that aren't going to require any major investment.

 Turn to **exercise fourteen** to work out your ROI for a gap you want to address.

First, add up all the returns and then subtract all the costs. Hopefully, you get a positive number here.

If not, did you factor in every possible benefit or return? For instance, if you identified something for compliance or safety as a risk that needs to be addressed, did you factor in cash flows from continuing to run your business as a benefit or return on your investment? If an employee slips and gets hurt, how much could that potentially cost you, especially since you are now aware of some unsafe working condition? Cost avoidance can be considered a return.

Now, some of these estimations may be fuzzy for what you're measuring. How exactly does someone measure employee happiness in terms of dollars? One easy way is to estimate increased productivity (revenue gain). Or, you could factor in the cost to replace an employee if they leave because they're unhappy (cost avoidance).

After all of this, you may have come up with a negative number, which means you shouldn't pursue that particular project. For most of what you've identified, that shouldn't be a big deal, and hey, now you have facts to present to your employees when they question why you aren't buying that new copier. For others, like major safety or compliance investments, it may be time to reassess your business model or even consider an exit strategy.

Julie:

I had a client who needed help with her leadership team. She had a team of six C-Level direct reports, and there was a lot of divisiveness within the team. Honestly, the entire business was a mix of chaos, drama, and good selling.

One of the C-Level executives was notorious for essentially making up numbers. Week after week, this exec would sit in leadership meetings and throw out data points to fit the narrative she was pitching on that particular day. One week, she provided data points to emphasize how much product was being stolen to cover her team's inefficiencies. When questioned about her numbers, she had no concrete reports or references to prove the point. Another week, she was pushing an agenda that the sales team wasn't hitting their targets. When the Chief Sales Officer pulled up a report to refute her claims, she resorted to arguing that she was talking about something else. Every week was a new story with no real data.

As much as I would love to give more examples (because I still laugh today at the memory of those conversations) the takeaway from this is that you need to do the analysis and then use a standard approach to measure. Don't make up numbers to prove your point; that won't help your business. And if you're truly stuck about how to approach this, then ask for help. Math nerds are everywhere. My co-author is one.

While creating fuzzy estimations may seem like making up numbers, it isn't if you have solid and reasonable logic to back it up. You may need to defend your estimations when using these to apply for a loan, so keep them realistic.

Now that you have estimations, it's time to start building that business case. You won't need to create a business case for small gaps, but you should develop the habit of creating a business case for significant changes. If you're making a big decision like expanding the footprint of your operation, you need a business case.

A business case is a simple way to ensure you have thought of everything when addressing gaps. Here are a few things to consider when building your business case:

- **Alternatives**—If you can't fill the gap, are there other things you can do that fix the problem another way? Most problems have more than one solution, and you should think each through with each to determine the best course of action as well as a fall back.

- **Ease of implementation**—How easy will it be to implement this? You should know off the top of your head whether or not this will be as simple as a company-wide email to address policy change or if it will require multiple departments and outside resources months to complete.

- **What happens if you don't fill the gap?**—This is pretty straightforward. You know what the gap is and the impact on your business as-is, but what does or will it cost you if you don't address the gap?

- **Likelihood of occurrence**—You'll want to estimate the likelihood of something breaking in your process due to a gap identified. For example, during your review you realized that one particular employee is holding an entire critical process together. If they were to win the lottery, what would that do to your business? How likely are they to win the lottery?

Turn back to **exercise fourteen** in the workbook to complete your business case. Fill in the considerations from above and look at the whole picture including the ROI. This should give you a much clearer picture of cost/benefit as well as potential impact on your business.

For now, your final step is to prioritize those gaps. Because everyone's circumstances are different, there's no wrong way to approach this, but this is where you need to determine the opportunity cost of addressing one gap versus another. You have to do it in a way that makes the most sense to you based upon ROI, timeliness, ease to implement, etc. You may have a large ROI if you purchase a new piece of technology, but it could potentially expose your business financially. Instead of purchasing that expensive technology, you could possibly address a handful of the other smaller gaps and have a larger combined ROI. This is where your experience as the business owner comes into play.

Don't let all of this ROI and business case talk deter you from addressing your "nice to haves." They don't have to be put on the back burner until you hit all the "need to haves." If you have a "nice to have" that costs next to nothing in time or money, why not implement it now?

What would I change if I had a
MAGIC WAND

In the mid-2000's Robert De Niro starred in the movie *The Intern* with Anne Hathaway. Hathaway's character owned an online clothing company and they had a company program to hire senior interns. Not seniors in high school or college, but seniors in life. The story mainly takes place in an old warehouse that has been converted into an open floor plan office space, completely trendy, and full of all the start-up vibes. Throughout the early part of the movie, there is a reference to this "junk desk," which drives Hathaway's character crazy. It's the equivalent of your junk drawer at home; only it's in plain sight for everyone to see, and you have 100 people stacking things on it.

With each passing day, Hathaway's character grows increasingly annoyed with the books and papers and boxes carelessly piled five feet in the air on this desk. She grimaces each time she passes the desk, but she never makes the time to clean it up. Finally, De Niro's character—the senior intern—comes in early one day and organizes the entire area, and the problem is solved. (Of course, in real life, we know that desk would be stacked up again with boxes and papers within two weeks, but in the movie, the problem was solved forever.)

Hathaway could have fixed that problem the minute it started to irritate her. And we will grant you this, that's a pretty easy problem to fix. Most people wouldn't waste a wish or the wave of a magic wand to handle something so mundane, but most people also don't realize they can fix things by pausing long enough to acknowledge the problem or by making some changes.

Is there something about your business that irritates you? If you're like most business owners, it doesn't take you long to come up with a short list of things you would love to change.

Maybe it's a staffing issue: you end up filling in as a support person for your sales team because you can't justify hiring someone to perform that job. Or, maybe your irritant is a customer that you have had since the business opened: they are a large and loyal customer, but they ask for a discount or refund on every purchase made and take up way too much of your time. Issues can run the gamut, so think of all facets of your business.

Start thinking about what you'd like to change if you could just wave that wand. It's a pretty straightforward process, so we skipped an exercise here. But to help get you thinking, here are some places to start:

- What is your customer experience like?

- How smooth is your onboarding process for new hires?

- Do your employees receive regular reviews?

- Are your processes documented?

- How do you train your employees on new technology or processes?

- How do you set annual goals?

- What's the process for giving feedback to employees?

- How do you communicate information to your team?

- What's your rewards and recognition program for employees?

- Are your offices clean and organized?

The possibilities of what you can evaluate are endless, and the chances are good that you don't need to give this area a lot of thought. You know the things that drive you crazy, but not so crazy that you're moved to do anything about them today. It's also possible that you're making excuses for why you aren't addressing the issue: "I have more important things to work on" or "The new point of sale system is too expensive."

Addressing these irritants before a crisis can help your business to run smoother during one. It also frees you up to focus on the big picture if you can knock these things out.

Corey:

I went back to visit a friend and previous employer at a restaurant where I used to work after college. I helped open the restaurant and had the "pleasure" of managing the business through the lean building years. He was walking me through all the changes he had made since I left years before, and one of the policies he implemented was to have a hostess on the clock during all business hours. While I was managing, we ran our labor numbers as tight as possible because we couldn't afford any extra expense, so we generally only had a hostess on the clock during busy hours on busy nights. That led to many issues during slower times when we allowed customers to seat themselves. By increasing the payroll by an almost insignificant amount in the grand scheme, he was able to free up his wait staff to focus on things that they should be focusing on, like upselling beverages. This change ultimately improved the customer experience because there was no longer an issue with people sitting and going unnoticed.

This concept brings us back to the return on investment for your opportunities. Sure, you could save a few hundred dollars a week by keeping your labor numbers tight. But what could you make if you were fully staffed and able to focus on those things that truly add value?

Tips for
SOLOPRENEURS

As a solopreneur, one area you'll want to pay close attention to is external gaps. Where do you depend on external resources or processes? Internally, you're going to be well aware of gaps because you're likely doing everything yourself. So it's important that you spend a few minutes thinking externally and going outside your business.

07 KNOW YOURSELF

"Tough times never last, but tough people do."
— Robert H. Schuller, Motivational Speaker

Julie:

We have talked about the importance of knowing your strengths and weaknesses. You not only need to know them, but you need to be honest with yourself about them. It's easy to highlight the strengths, believing if you focus on those, the weaknesses won't matter as much. But weaknesses have a way of showing themselves at the most inopportune times.

Occasionally, Corey and I like to do some hiking on the weekends. I'm not going to lie, hiking with Corey is challenging because he's a speed walker. He never meanders. He's always walking with a purpose, even in situations where walking slowly is the purpose, like leisurely walking with friends amongst stalls at a street fair. Now, add to his speed walking a mountain and it's tough. I'm usually sweating profusely (and cursing under my breath) within the first 15 minutes of the hike.

On a late spring day, we decided to hike Old Rag Mountain in Shenandoah National Park. We made the plans over text messages and Corey said, "It's a moderate hike. It's long but not overly difficult." I was in. A little background: there are few people in this world I trust more than Corey, so when he says it's a long but moderate hike, I believe him.

Well, the moderately difficult hike was 9.1 miles. Okay, so he had told me upfront it was a long hike. What he failed to tell me was that there was a 2400-feet in elevation gain and that the last 1.5 miles on the way up are a rock scramble. If you're not familiar with a rock scramble, you're basically taking your life into your own hands and at any moment a fall to your death is possible.

I was scared out of my mind. And physically tired from the hike we'd already completed. And I didn't believe I had the physical strength to complete the rock scramble. My anxiety was through the roof. I followed him from rock to rock, using his hand and foot placement as my guide, many times so fearful that I thought I was going to throw-up.

On the way up the mountain, we talked excitedly about the hike, and I told Corey about my nerves and my fear of not succeeding. Having the awareness that I likely had an internal struggle with my ability to climb the mountain, Corey stepped in with a little "cheerleading." He started telling me, "We're almost to the top," and with each turn, I'd become more frustrated because the top was nowhere in sight. I finally said, "I need you to stop telling me that we are almost to the top if we aren't because I don't ever want to be in a situation on this mountain where I don't trust you. I wouldn't make it to the top if I stopped trusting you." After that, he stopped saying, "We're almost there."

My weakness on that mountain wasn't my physical strength or even my extreme fear of falling to my death. My weakness was my self-talk. The dialogue I was having in my head was my single biggest battle. Corey knew that, so with each complicated scramble I completed, he assured me that I could do the next one. If I had known what climbing Old Rag Mountain entailed before we went, I might have mentally prepared myself, but I also would have very likely been more anxious about it. Not knowing was a benefit for me. Corey counted on me not doing my own research. More importantly, he counted on the fact that I trusted him enough to follow him through it.

Now, as a result, I am hyper-aware of my self-talk and I work daily on controlling my internal bully.

Why knowing yourself is
IMPORTANT

Being self-aware is not a quality that everyone is blessed with. We see lack of self-awareness play out every single day from folks driving s-l-o-w-l-y in the fast lane while 27 cars stack up behind them to people who play music on their iPhones in public...without headphones. While it's maddening when people seem so unaware of others, we all can slip into these behaviors. That's why we're devoting some time to this topic: it's imperative that you be self-aware as a business owner.

Being self-aware is more than understanding how your actions impact others; it's about how it impacts you and your business. It's about knowing who you are. The two of us aren't therapists (even though it feels like it sometimes), but let's talk about you.

How to identify your personal
STRENGTHS AND WEAKNESSES

You're likely in tune with some of your strengths and weaknesses, which means there's an opportunity to learn more. A simple approach to identifying what is in each category is to create a list.

 You guessed it. We have an exercise in the workbook! Flip to **exercise fifteen** to get started.

In the left-hand column, you'll find a space to do a brain dump of all of your personal strengths. This part may be easy for some, and there's nothing wrong with healthy self-esteem, so go ahead and list out your strengths. If you're having trouble, try compartmentalizing different areas of your life such as your family, friendships, and hobbies and see if that makes it easier. If you consider yourself to be a loving father, you may be a compassionate leader. If you find yourself making lists of things that need to be done around the house, maybe you're organized. If it seems that all of your friends call you when they want to vent, you're probably a good listener. You could also reflect back on compliments you may have received for additional strengths. Write everything down that you can think of.

Julie:

Now repeat this for the right-hand column: your weaknesses. For those of you who may find this section difficult, think about those things that take you longer to complete or that you avoid doing at all (or just ask your mother-in-law). Having a weakness shouldn't be something you're ashamed of. For example, I am great at building personal relationships and communicating, whereas Corey struggles in this area. In some cases, you may want to work on a weakness you have, but there will be situations where it's fine for weaknesses to remain just that. Because building relationships is a strength for me, I focus on everything external such as sales and marketing, and Corey spends more time on those things that are more internal. If there's someone else on the team who is more suited to do a particular task than you let them do it. (Unless it's running the company, in which case, you may need to pick up a different book.)

Here's a quick example of a Strengths and Weaknesses table:

STRENGTHS	WEAKNESSES
• Organized • Good listener • Excellent communicator • Strong leadership • Compassionate • Microsoft Office • Sales • Marketing • Team building • Leadership development	• Multi-tasking • Tend to hold grudges • Don't like to be challenged • Trust issues • Communicate too much via email • Struggle to be productive in the mornings • Stubborn at times • Math

One final piece of advice for identifying strengths and weaknesses: ask those close to you for their thoughts! But don't be upset with the responses if you don't like them. As a general rule, don't ask for someone's input and then fly off the handle when you don't like what you hear. (If that's your reaction to feedback, you should write that down in the weakness column, and we recommend reading *Thanks for the Feedback: The Science and Art of Receiving Feedback* by Douglas Stone and Sheila Heen.)

If you don't feel like you have anyone who will give you feedback openly, then we suggest you complete an anonymous 360 review with your team. A quick Internet search will return plenty of options.

Personal **STRENGTHS AND WEAKNESSES** *versus those of* your **BUSINESS**

It's important to be clear about the difference between personal strengths and weaknesses and the strengths and weaknesses of the business itself.

Corey and Julie:

We have a client who is so strong at selling that she could close a deal with anyone. It's her superpower. We frequently watch in amazement as she turns a "no" into a "yes." She accomplishes this by providing a lot of detail, asking a ton of questions, being available 24-7, and frequently checking in on her prospects. She handles her personal relationships the same way. She sometimes calls her friends five or six times a day. She texts relentlessly. In her friendships, it's what makes people push the calls to voicemail. In business, that level of attention is what makes her great.

The strengths of your business exist because of you and what you have built. It also includes your team and what they bring to the table. The knowledge and expertise, your customer's perception, and your financial strength exist because of a combination of you and your team. Wanting to make your business more of an extension of you isn't wrong, just make sure it fits what you're trying to sell. Imagine if you were a health coach who was 100 lbs. overweight. It's going to be difficult for you to sell "health" to others if you're not healthy yourself. We're not saying it can't be done, but we are saying that it's going to be extremely challenging.

How do you
HANDLE FEEDBACK?

Do you welcome feedback from others? Are you willing to accept both positive and negative feedback?

How do you provide feedback to others? Do you give it generously? Do you position the feedback in a way that makes it easier to receive?

Giving and receiving feedback is an art and one that most folks could stand to practice.

As a small business owner, you should strive to create a culture that encourages two-way feedback. Such a culture will help you during a crisis, as people will more willingly give and receive feedback at a time when every move is critical.

Telling someone they need to work on an area can be hard, and chances are it's as difficult for the person giving the feedback as it is for the person receiving it. But, the ability to give feedback to others that helps them to grow and develop is important in both professional and personal lives.

Receiving feedback isn't easy if you get defensive when it happens, or if you brush off positive accolades with a shrug and an "oh, it's nothing" type of attitude. When you're the leader of a company, your employees are less likely to give you feedback, not because you don't need it but because there's an intimidation factor. If your employees don't know how you'll respond to criticism or if they think there may be repercussions, they probably won't provide it. Build a company culture that welcomes feedback or constructive compliments.

How do you
LEAD OTHERS?

Why does leadership style matter? The short answer is that the way you lead others impacts your business.

So, what is your leadership style? Be honest with yourself. Do you hang out at happy hours with your team, or do you rule with an iron fist? A friendly, collaborative leadership style is great for some companies, but it doesn't work for all. If you own a personal security company, you're probably more rigid than someone who runs a hipster coffee shop. Your style should fit your business. That doesn't mean the owner of the personal security business shouldn't be available to employees if they need help or have feedback. It means that the personal security business owner needs to ensure policies are followed because people's lives are at risk.

Get intimate with your leadership style and then consider surrounding yourself with people who complement that style. Look at your strengths and weaknesses and then compare with your business to find any similarities or gaps. If you like to control everything, work with people who will constructively push back or question you. If you aren't good at marketing, consider hiring an outside firm to handle that. Even if you are a company of one or two people, how you lead others is still important. It's still a piece of the puzzle. You are leading not only employees, but you're leading customers and possibly competitors.

Now that you're familiar with yourself and leadership style, it's time to understand how you lead under pressure.

Corey:

I was hired to manage a small coffee shop a few months after it had opened. I had years of high-paced, high-stress bar experience under my belt, but the quick service coffee world was new to me. No matter, my experience could translate. The previous manager apparently could not handle stress well, and the owner was frankly a bit of a tyrant. As a result, the employees were always on edge.

One particularly busy Saturday morning, it was just me and one other barista behind the counter while patrons stacked up. She was panicking about the line of customers waiting to place their order, about how something needed to be restocked, about this, about that. I stopped her and asked, "Do I look stressed right now? Am I concerned about the dishes? No, and you shouldn't be either." We made it through the shift, the customers were served promptly, and she and I chatted afterward. She said that I helped her because I wasn't a high-strung mess yelling at everyone. My calm approach to providing customer service in a high-stress environment rubbed off on her.

Leading during a crisis is different than leading when times are good. How you react could impact your business beyond the end of that crisis. If you demonstrate confidence and keep a level head, you'll likely reach the other side with employees who respect you more. Lose your head or disappear from sight, and you will likely lose their confidence in you and potentially lose them altogether.

Unknowns require leaders to show up, take charge, and make decisions quickly. Sometimes that decision is to turn leadership over to the person better suited to handling a crisis. Asking someone else to lead during a crisis is fine, just make that decision confidently. Learn who you are and how you lead today, so there are no surprises tomorrow.

The leadership
YOUR COMPANY NEEDS REGULARLY

As your company moves through different stages, the type of leader needed may change. How you lead when the company is starting up can be very different from the type of leadership needed when you hit 100 employees and revenues are through the roof. It's also possible that you are more than prepared to lead in both of those situations, but you have to recognize that the way you lead could be very different.

Initially, you're working in the business. You're right next to your small team doing all the things necessary to drive that new business to success. You're working *in* the business. But, as the company grows and you become more successful, your focus may shift to potentially working exclusively *on* the business, the vision, and the brand. Your leadership style may have to be flexible.

Building a team, satisfying your customers, setting and hitting sales goals, and building a culture that attracts the right talent to your company are examples of areas where leaders need to focus, and how those are prioritized may shift over time.

You should be so aware of what your company needs from a leadership perspective that you are able to adjust your style as the company grows and changes. One of the biggest challenges facing any leader of a growing business is delegation of duties. It is often hard to relinquish control over something you lived and breathed for so long, but you can't grow if you can't trust your team to run the day-to-day minutia.

The **LEADERSHIP** *your company* *needs* **DURING A CRISIS**

It takes a confident, courageous, self-aware leader to step back and let someone else lead, especially in a crisis. When you find yourself in the thick of a crisis, pause to ask yourself what the company needs most right now. What type of leadership? What strengths can you leverage to move the company in the right direction? What weaknesses do you have that someone else can help offset?

This isn't that uncommon, so don't feel like you're a weak leader if this is something that you believe is necessary.

Corey and Julie:

A company we worked for in California had their operations manager as the safety manager, which included responding to earthquakes. So, if there happened to be a serious earthquake, the president of the company was essentially no longer in charge. Everything defaulted to the safety manager's discretion. Sure, the president of the company could have educated himself to learn those duties, but he had much more important things to do. So, he appointed one of his managers to fill that role.

If you're facing a crisis and you're unsure if you're the right person to lead, ask yourself some hard questions. Be able to quickly determine if you're the best person to lead. If you're not, get to know your team well enough (covered in the next chapter) to know who can lead. And if you're asking someone else to lead, have a strategy for how it's going to work.

Exercise sixteen in your workbook is designed to help you work through leadership options for your business during a crisis. Ask yourself the following:

- Who will communicate during the crisis?

- When will you resume full leadership?

- What information will you provide your employees?

- What exactly is it that they're leading?

- Is this a co-leadership approach? If so, who is leading what?

- How will you support the new leader?

Having a strategy in place before it's needed, even if it's a simple outline of things you'll need to know before the change is implemented, will strengthen the approach and give you the confidence to execute successfully.

If you're in a crisis and you know that the leadership and direction of someone else on the team, if more appropriate at that time, be transparent with your employees. It's not a sign of weakness to step back, and your employees will support the decision if you're up front about it.

Many organizations have someone in the role of crisis manager (or safety manager). Generally speaking, being a crisis manager isn't a full-time role but rather a role that someone on the team fills on an as-needed basis. And it's safe to say that we hope that need isn't too frequent.

Here are some tips on communicating effectively with your team when you're putting someone else in charge:

- **Demonstrate confidence**—Be clear about what the business needs most right now, and be confident in asking for leadership from others on the team.

- **Be honest**—In a crisis, people look to leadership for information and guidance. Provide both. Be honest about how you're going to lead them through the crisis, even if that means you're asking someone else to lead.

- **Create a new plan**—If this is something you haven't experienced or planned for, determine what existing plan(s) you could modify to fit this scenario.

- **Leverage emotional intelligence**—Double down on it. Lead with empathy and support. And if you can't do that, find the person on your team who can, because in a crisis people need it.

What's your
MOTIVATION?

Julie:

In the fall of 2019, I went to a business conference that had an incredible line-up of speakers. The conference was built around the concept of getting your business to the next level regardless of its current state. Over three days, I jotted down a lot of inspiring quotes as well as actions I could take immediately to get some traction.

The speaker who resonated the most with me was Tom Bilyeu, the co-founder of both Quest Nutrition and Impact Theory. He talked about having to work hard, work smart, and work long hours to build something that matters. He highlighted the importance of constantly learning new things to take your business to the next level. But what imprinted the most on my brain is this: *"The struggle is guaranteed. The success is not. You better love the f*cking struggle!"*

Owning a small business IS a struggle. There is no question you have had days when you asked yourself, "Why am I doing this?" Yet every day, you show up and start again.

What's your "why"? Maybe you don't want to go back to the corporate world. Maybe you produce some delicious but healthy treat, and your passion is to make people healthier. Maybe you own a retail store and love the social aspect of customer interactions. It could be the money you do or could make. There are a lot of reasons to own a business. It's personal, and there isn't a right or wrong answer. But understanding what keeps you coming into work every day helps you prepare for when a crisis hits.

We know plenty of people in the corporate world whose "why" is that they have a family to provide for. They're essentially there to pick up a paycheck. That's fine in the office grind where you can squeak by with the bare minimum and a crappy attitude towards work (and your co-workers), but that won't fly in small business. If you are in business to make money, make sure there is still some passion for what you provide. If there isn't, your customers and staff will know.

Pressures
OUTSIDE OF WORK

We're sure there's an exception to this, but it's safe to assume that you have a life outside of work, and that most likely means at least one other person, creature, or thing requires your attention. Whether that's a spouse, kids, parents, friends, college buddies, your house and lawn, your dog, or something else, there is an outside force that wants some of your time and energy.

We all know how stress works: it's a drain on our energy and health. To minimize stress, you need a strategy to combat it. Stress requires attention. Ideally, your solution for balancing your stress is something healthy, like working out, reading, getting enough sleep, taking regular time off, or spending time doing things you enjoy that aren't work-related. There are plenty of options available, so find one or two (or three) that work for you.

Be aware of how pressures outside of work impact your life. Most folks aren't great at separating their business from their personal life, so if you're getting pressure at home to spend more time with the kids or deal with personal financial issues, it's most likely going to show up in how you run the business. It's also likely to show up in how you treat yourself. Having strategies for dealing with stress and outside pressures will make you stronger for dealing with a crisis at work.

The best solution is to remove external pressure as best you can, but we understand that it isn't possible to do completely. If you can't remove it, be aware of it and have a strategy for how you handle it. Even this slight change will help you focus better during a crisis at work.

When to
ASK FOR HELP

We have focused on *you*, the leader, exclusively in this chapter. You have performed a lot of self-reflection, and if you have completed the exercises, you know yourself better which positions you to be a better leader.

Owning a business doesn't mean knowing how to do and handle everything. Assuming you've already tapped all of the resources you have within your business, you should be ready to reach out to external resources. A simple Internet search now could save you a ton of time down the road. There are groups on social media you could join, or you could reach out to business coaches or small business consulting services now to help strengthen your plan. Help is out there in a variety of forms. Don't be afraid or ashamed to ask for help when you need it. You are an expert in what you do, and sometimes asking for help from someone with a fresh pair of eyes is required. That help could come from someone in your industry or a different one; the key is getting a different perspective.

Even if you're running the most successful business possible, you can't know everything. When you hit a wall and the Internet can't answer the question, try using the phone for what it was originally invented for and make a call.

Tips for
SOLOPRENEURS

Even though you're a team of one, these exercises have value. Having a thorough understanding of your strengths and weaknesses, how you handle feedback and how you lead others are all important to know, even if you are the only person working in your business. As long as you have customers, understanding this information about yourself will strengthen your business.

We recommend that you find someone in your network that you feel comfortable with and ask for some direct feedback. Don't ask your mom because moms are usually too nice. Ask a former boss or even better, ask someone who you used to manage. Regardless of who you ask, the critical element here is that you have somebody who will give you open and honest feedback.

08 KNOW YOUR PEOPLE

> "The strength of the team is each individual member. The strength of each member is the team."
> — Phil Jackson, NBA Head Coach

Corey:

I had a conversation with a former Navy SEAL about his experiences in the military. Aside from his many crazy combat stories, he spoke a lot about his team and how tight they were. They spent almost every hour of every day together, and they had to so that they could work as one instead of as individuals. He said they knew each other so well that they could tell each other apart in almost pitch-black conditions simply by the way someone walked.

What it means to know
YOUR EMPLOYEES

You spent **CHAPTER 7: KNOW YOURSELF** focusing inward, and now it's time to turn the focus outward to look at your employees. This chapter dives deep into what it means to know your employees, why it's important, and how it can benefit you.

At its most basic, knowing your employees means understanding their roles, their strengths, and their weaknesses. Having this information allows you to act quickly, and it allows you to be intentional in your day to day operations as you work your strategic plans. That's a big advantage for recovering quickly or making pivots.

Corey:

When it came to scheduling servers in restaurants I managed, the best ones got the best shifts. Pretty simple. But it wasn't always that easy. I had to not only balance abilities, I had to balance personalities. Certain servers didn't work well with other servers, and some servers were only great when it was busy—they were great at working tables, upselling, etc. but they would fall apart if the support staff of bussers and hostesses weren't there to pick up their slack. I had to know exactly who I was scheduling and how each would add or detract from that team on that particular shift.

Knowing your employees doesn't mean knowing about their home lives or how they like to spend their weekends. You don't have to talk about favorite movies or their favorite class in college. You can take it to that level if that's your leadership style, but what matters is understanding how you can leverage employees beyond their current roles should the need arise.

If you don't personally have the bandwidth to know your employees at this level, then leverage your management team. Sometimes it's not possible to know all of your employees, and if you're leading the company, you have to think about the ROI of personally knowing every detail about every employee.

Note: If you are the type of leader who likes to engage on a more personal level with your employees, make sure that it doesn't get misconstrued and turned into a lawsuit. The last thing you want to deal with is an employee filing a harassment complaint because you keep asking them about their workouts at the gym.

Why knowing your
EMPLOYEES IS IMPORTANT

In every company we have ever worked for, we have witnessed leaders leverage the strengths of direct reports for special projects, pivots, and even crises. Almost always, it's the leader calling on the same individuals over and over again. They have a few strong managers whom they trust and know can complete any task thrown at them. The rest of the team isn't leveraged in the same manner. Imagine the benefit to the organization if leaders were able to call upon their entire staff when needed.

We are certain you know the obvious benefit of leveraging an entire staff: businesses could react more efficiently if they had more resources available when they needed to shift. Another benefit is that it increases employee loyalty. People want to work for leaders who openly value them. If you understand what your people do, trust your managers to use all of their resources, and find ways to leverage skills outside of your team's regular roles, your employees are going to feel valued. That's a huge benefit that you get simply because you know your employees.

Bottom line is this: Knowing your employees allows you to respond quickly to change, it provides you the opportunity to pivot when needed, and it builds loyalty in your team. If you have a team with multiple levels, challenge managers and supervisors to know their people. There may be skills or personalities in your organization that you should know about in case a crisis occurs.

Get to know
YOUR EMPLOYEES

Ideally, there isn't anything listed here that you aren't already doing. We include this as a reminder because it can be easy to forget how important it is to know your team.

- **Team meetings**—Regularly cadenced team meetings provide an opportunity to have small snippets of casual conversation. Julie always started her team meetings with an "ice breaker" question—something fun to not only lighten the mood but to get people thinking outside of the box. The questions ranged from "What's the best invention ever?" to "What's your superpower?" Getting to know your team doesn't have to be clinical, and your team would probably prefer it if it weren't.

- **Talk to them individually**—You can gather a lot of information about an employee simply by having a conversation. If this isn't obvious, go back to **CHAPTER 7: KNOW YOURSELF** and start over about how you lead.

- **Reviews**—The highest performing teams we have ever worked with did quarterly assessments in addition to annual reviews. This book isn't about building high performing teams, but there's a benefit to having a team full of high performers when a crisis hits. Regardless, performing regular reviews will benefit all employees, including you. Pay attention to how employees view their strengths because that could provide insight into the direction they may want to take their career, or it could be an indication of work they enjoy doing.

- **Self-assessments**—Self-assessments are a useful tool if you want to have a better understanding of how employees view themselves. While an employee will provide feedback on their performance during quarterly and annual reviews, a self-assessment tends to go deeper, allowing the employee to provide even greater insight into not only their strengths and weaknesses but what their future goals are.

- **360 assessments**—If you can have team members assess each other, you will find yourself with a great deal of helpful information. People pay close attention to how other members of the team work. They know which person to go to for help building out formulas in Excel and who to ask for help running a meeting. They know who builds relationships with ease and who doesn't finish their assignments on time. If you want to know what's really going on with your team, do 360 reviews.

Employee
STRENGTHS AND WEAKNESSES

When you looked at your personal strengths and weaknesses in **CHAPTER 7: KNOW YOURSELF**, it was to give you additional insight into when and where you may need help to not only run your business but to also lead through a crisis. Knowing what strengths and weaknesses your employees have gives you the ability to respond quicker in any emergency because it allows you to put people in the right position to help.

You can use any of the approaches listed in *Get to Know My Employees* (above) for a starting point. Your employees can complete the same Strengths and Weaknesses exercise you did in **CHAPTER 7: KNOW YOURSELF.** We have always found the easiest way to get information from someone is to ask them.

Once you have the information, use it. Don't wait for a crisis to leverage your team members' strengths. Improve your business starting today and then keep the information close so that you can continue to use it over time.

Know your
CRITICAL FUNCTIONS AND WHO DOES THEM

In **CHAPTER 4: PROCESS ANALYSIS,** you learned the importance of knowing and documenting the critical processes for your business. From that information, you should have a solid understanding of what your critical functions are—those things that are necessary for your business to operate.

An example would be getting your product to your customer. The method of delivery isn't necessarily important as there are most likely options (use your own fleet, 3rd party carrier, have the customer pick it up, etc.). You may have to create multiple plans for each, but what is critical is that the customer receives the product they ordered when they wanted it.

For every critical function identified, know who the primary person is—whoever completes the function—as well as who performs any backup. If you have a task being performed by a certain employee, and one day she quits without notice, you're going to need to hand off all of her work. Make it easier on yourself by having at least one other person trained on the critical functions that person performs. You can't predict what will happen with your employees, and you don't want your lack of preparedness to result in not being able to function as a business. That back-up doesn't have to be the expert that your former employee was, but they should be knowledgeable about the processes and have confidence in performing them.

 Open your workbook to **exercise seventeen** and list out who performs your critical functions and whoever might be a backup for that role.

While critical functions are being covered, it's time to mention again the importance of documenting them. You don't know what's going to happen with your people. Everyone likes to believe they are hiring the right people, but the reality is that as long as you're dealing with humans, you're dealing with unpredictability. So, until you can fully staff your team with robots, be prepared for someone walking out the door without notice. (And, if the movies taught us anything, even robots are unpredictable.)

Roles and
RESPONSIBILITIES

Part of knowing your people is knowing what responsibilities they have in their roles. Knowing what each employee does is part of being a good leader, but it also provides you with data points during critical times. If revenue is down and you have to lay people off, use all of the information available to you to make decisions. This includes employee reviews, stack rankings, strengths/weaknesses, and roles/responsibilities.

You want to know everything a person is working on and all of their responsibilities before you start letting people go. Unless you are closing your doors permanently, someone needs to do the work, and you may not want that responsibility to fall on you.

If you're a lean business that doesn't have a lot of extra bandwidth, get creative, especially if you're starting from zero.

Here are some options and approaches:

- Did you create a job description when you hired your employees? If you did, then start with that as a baseline for the responsibilities of the respective roles.

- Create a bulleted list. You don't have to create something super formal; it can be quick and easy, and you can add to it over time.

- Have employees document what they do. Not every function is completed every day, so give employees 30 to 45 days to complete the task. You'll have a well-documented job description once they are done.

- The job descriptions may have changed along with your business, so you may need to review them. It's also possible that your team is performing tasks that you're unaware of. That's okay. If they're autonomous, you shouldn't worry, but you should continue to ask them to update what it is that they're doing.

- Review the roles and responsibilities annually. You don't have to spend hours on each role, but a quick walk-through while you're doing an employee review could help you better define your business.

Note: If employee reviews and job description updates aren't things that regularly occur, you might end up with paranoid employees who think they're about to be let go. Be honest and transparent about your intentions.

Have the right
PEOPLE IN THE RIGHT ROLES

Part of running a business is putting the right people in the right roles to position yourself for success. When a crisis occurs, your definition of success looks very different. If you owned a business in 2008 or 2020, then you know what it's like to fight for your life as a small business. You may need to shift people around when a crisis hits.

Here are a few questions you should be asking:

- Is this the team I would want by my side if the biggest crisis imaginable happened?

- If I needed to pivot my business quickly, do I have the right people on my team to do that?

- Do I trust the people working for me?

Hiring and building a team requires skill, art, and luck. There is no bulletproof formula for building the absolute right team for your organization. So, like we advised when you performed a SWOT, be honest with yourself about your team.

Corey:

> At a restaurant I managed after college, I had one barback (the person who supports the bartenders) who was amazing at his job. Everything was stocked to the perfect amount—not too much and not too little. The second I ran out of something and went to reach for more, he was there handing me that exact thing I needed. It was almost uncanny. So, it made sense that he would be a great bartender as well, and he was, just not when it was busy.
>
> He was attentive and great at conversation, but he didn't have that hustle we needed during the prime shifts. Even though he was the best barback for busy nights and weekends, that didn't translate into being a good volume bartender. We talked, and he understood why he wasn't getting a better bartender schedule. But, we didn't want to lose him, so he was probably the highest-paid barback in town.

Put the right people in the right roles.

Helpful **TIPS:**

- Utilize employees who have a military, law enforcement, or any kind of emergency services background. They've been trained in responding to bad situations, so you could possibly leverage that and put them in charge of disaster management. For most small businesses, this isn't a full-time role, so it wouldn't be a big ask.

- Update information on employee roles and responsibilities at least once a year. People leave. New people are hired. Skills improve, keep it fresh.

Employee
REVIEWS

If ever there was a polarizing activity in the workplace, this is it. People either love or hate review time. The "Performance Review" episode of *The Office* (Season 2, Episode 8) gives us a humorous look at the annual process.

The experiences are relatable, from Pam not being sure what to expect: *"It's performance review day, company-wide. Last year, my performance review started with Michael asking me what my hopes and dreams were, and it ended with him telling me he could bench-press 190 pounds. So, I don't really know what to expect."* ...to Angela being excited about the annual event: *"I actually look forward to performance reviews. I did the youth beauty pageant circuit. And I enjoyed that quite a bit. I really enjoy being judged. I believe I hold up very well to even severe scrutiny."*

We're going to assume that our readers aren't working for Michael Scott at the Dunder Mifflin Paper Company and that the review process is taken more seriously, even if only ever so slightly.

Employee reviews are important for several reasons. First, they are an opportunity for two-way communication between managers and employees. They also provide leaders with comprehensive information on how every employee within the company is performing. They give employees a chance to self-assess and identify where they are struggling and where they can take on more responsibility. They provide a vehicle for implementing performance improvement plans (PIPs) for struggling employees if needed. And they are usually used as the basis for pay increases.

While the review itself is generally considered annoying and time-consuming, employees usually comply, even if it means sending them multiple reminders of the approaching due date. We have personally found that when reviews are completed regularly, it sets expectations for employees and pushes them to perform better throughout the entire year.

When you're doing reviews, you should also consider completing a stack ranking exercise. Stack ranking was developed in the mid-'80s by then-CEO Jack Welch as an important exercise to perform for understanding the overall value add and performance of your team. But, we are not suggesting that you stack rank your employees and then put the bottom 20% of them on PIPs as Welch did. We are recommending you complete stack rankings to have another tool available to you should the need arise to lay employees off during an economic downturn or some other crisis.

When completing stack rankings, you want to start at a team level, and then move out to eventually having a stack ranking for the organization. You can alter the criteria used for this exercise, but commonly you'll find employers rank based on one single question: Who is the most important employee I need to keep my critical processes functioning?

It's a focused question that cuts right to the heart of the goal and identifies what is most important for the business. Here is a sample approach you can use:

- **Step 1—Each manager ranks his/her team members.**
  Everyone must be ranked. Ask each manager to include themselves in the stack rankings of their respective teams.

- **Step2—Rank by department.** Have the department head lead this exercise. Managers will need to articulate (defend) their rankings against the other managers. But there shouldn't be any real surprises in how the final department rankings land. Note that you'll now be ranking the managers, who may be sitting in the room. An alternative approach would be to not include the managers in the rankings while they are in the room and have that occur with only the department head providing input.

- **Step 3—Rank by organization.** This ranking occurs between senior staff and you. Perform the same process as in step 2.

Once you finish step 3, you will have a completed stack ranking for every employee in your organization. The first time through the process is the most time-consuming. After that, it becomes easier as you'll likely only have slight changes, perhaps due to turnover or role changes within the company.

Depending on the size of your business, stack ranking may not be applicable, or it may be an informal process within your organization. If you only have 10-20 employees, you likely already know who your best and worst employees are and have performed an informal stack ranking. As long as you know which employees are critical to your business, you can keep this an informal process.

For what we hope are obvious reasons, you'll keep the stack ranking confidential. While we're sure some companies publish the rankings for all to see, our personal recommendation is that you keep them confidential. You don't need extra drama in your organization because someone is upset they're ranked below someone else even though they've been there longer. Keep the stack rankings with your employee reviews—under lock and key.

Note: We didn't include an exercise in the workbook for stack rankings because we want you to be able to share the workbook with your team without revealing anything too sensitive.

Rapid
ONBOARDING AND OFFBOARDING

As a leader, you may encounter crisis situations that require you to onboard and/or offboard a lot (possibly all) of your employees very quickly. Having a process documented to help you will ease this work. It doesn't need to be an overly formal process. You could create a quick checklist that you can use to ensure you haven't forgotten anything.

We suggest that you speak with an HR expert or your legal network to determine the best course of action in either scenario to protect yourself from any possible lawsuits. It may also be a good idea to get some advice from an accountant or financial expert as there may be benefits you can take advantage of. From all of your experts, you will need to know what the cost will be to onboard or offboard employees as additional costs outside of their pay, such as health care and other benefits, need to be factored in.

As much as we hate to say it, in the era of social media, it's important to get this part right. You don't need to face an angry online mob at the same time as you're dealing with a legitimate crisis in your business, so make sure your employees know that you're working in everyone's best interest. They need to know you're supporting them even if you had to let them go.

EXTERNAL SUPPORT

Professional SERVICES

Every small business is different in terms of the internal team (the people they employ) versus their external team (the people they pay for services). We realize that money may be an obstacle, so we encourage you to find the fit that's best for your company and to get creative where you can. The three most important are as follows:

- **Accountant** (watches your money) We talked about accountants in **CHAPTER FIVE: BUSINESS OPERATIONS** of the book, but it's possible if you're small, you don't have an accountant on your payroll. Your in-house bookkeeper could also double as your accountant, or maybe it makes sense to have a check-and-balance. Your call. One business we interviewed has an accountant who's on call. He does payroll, forecasting, files their taxes, and performs annual budgeting. They pay him a low monthly fee and he's available all year long for them. Explore options to see what's available to you to meet the needs of your business.

- **Attorney** (attempts to keep you out of jail) Unless you're writing contracts regularly, you probably don't need legal counsel available at your disposal. But, you should have a good attorney that you can consult when needed. At the very least, have the relationship established. You don't know when you're going to need someone, but when you do, you want it to be someone you know and already trust.

- **Marketing** (spins it so no one knows you went to jail) Having someone on your team who can manage your marketing is important. This is a job that needs dedicated attention. The occasional online post won't get much attention. You need someone who is creating and responding to social media. This doesn't need to be a full-time position, but it does need a dedicated resource. It could be a $15/hour college student/intern, or a $150,000/year marketing exec. That's your decision to make.

Support
NETWORK

Having a strong support network is important for anyone regardless of career, but for small business owners, it can be the difference between losing and keeping your business during a crisis. Outside of professional services and others with which you do business, this will include your friends and family. It's anyone you can reach out to for help or to talk through your situation.

When we interviewed small business owners for this book, we were in the early stages of COVID-19 and *shelter-in-place* throughout the United States. Nearly everything—schools, restaurants, gyms, dentist offices, daycare centers—had been shut down, and we were interested in how this impacted small businesses across all sectors. One particular interview highlighted the importance of having a support network.

Corey and Julie:

One client we spoke with is the owner of a hair salon in the state of Minnesota. The Governor had ordered all non-essential businesses closed about ten days before our conversation. Our client is the sole provider for her family, and shutting down her salon meant no income at all. The small business relief loans had yet to be created when this conversation occurred, so there was some level of panic.

During the hour or so we were on the phone, we focused on understanding her situation and talking through ideas for how she could pivot her business so she could still have income coming in the door. Because we weren't in the thick of her crisis, it was easier for us to think through pivots with this client.

Our client was initially fearful about what would happen to her business. She didn't believe she had any options, but talking through the problem with people who aren't connected to the business helped her realize that she did.

A global crisis isn't necessary to reach out to your own support network. There's no need to face things all alone when times get hard. Talking through situations or problems with someone who isn't in the trenches with you brings fresh insight. Leverage your support system.

If you're successful, people may want to take advantage of that by being near you to influence how you run your business and the decisions you make. Be wary of that. Don't fall victim to anyone because of blind loyalty. Make certain every person who has a voice in your business has the best interest of the business in mind and is there in good times and bad.

09 KNOW YOUR CUSTOMERS

> "There is only one boss: The customer. And he can fire everybody in the company from the chairman on down, simply by spending his money somewhere else."
> — Sam Walton, Founder of Walmart

One of the small business owners that we interviewed for this book is a masseuse with a loyal client following. Because her business depends on human touch, she was heavily impacted by the COVID-19 pandemic. She had to shut her business down with absolutely no idea when she would be allowed to open up again and what it would look like when she could.

This small business owner spoke so eloquently to us about how a business manages through crisis defines them. She was communicating regularly with her clients about what she knew. She carefully explained that she didn't know what the future would hold, but the safety and comfort of her clients was at the top of her priority list.

Knowing her customers made it easier for this small business owner to communicate effectively with her clients about what to expect in the future.

Your ideal
CUSTOMER AVATAR

You will start this chapter with an exercise building your ideal customer avatar. Don't worry, you won't have to draw anything. This is a fun exercise in getting to know who you should be targeting. When you invest the time to detail this out, it helps with a lot of decision making in the future. If you're stuck on marketing a product or service, look at your ideal customer. If you're unsure if a new product or service would sell, refer back to your avatar. It's a great tool that you will use again and again.

Even if you've already completed this exercise in the past, it's time to revisit it and examine what has changed.

Turn to **exercise eighteen** in the workbook and start working on the ideal customer avatar. Your avatar will be based on a single individual. This individual will come to represent the bulk of your customers. Here is a series of questions to get you started. You can go deeper, though. It isn't possible to list too much information. Everything helps.

Below are characteristics to consider on the list:

- Start by giving your ideal customer a name (if it helps, at SB PACE we call our ideal customer Bob)

- What age is your customer?

- Where does your customer live?

- Is your customer on social media? If yes, which platforms? If no, why not?

- What does your customer do for a living?

- How much money does your customer make annually?

- Is your customer married?

- Does your customer have children?

- What are the religious beliefs of your customer?

- What are the political beliefs of your customer?

- Is your customer physically fit?

- What hobbies does your customer enjoy?

- Where does your customer vacation?

This list is just the start of questions you can answer about your ideal customer, but you can go deeper. Try to find another five or six characteristics to add more detail to your avatar. Don't limit yourself to this list. Get your team together and spend 30 minutes asking and answering questions about your ideal customer.

What it means to
KNOW YOUR CUSTOMERS

Now it's time to widen the lens and think about your customers in more general terms, rather than focusing on your avatar. Let's talk about your customers' habits specific to your business. These next questions will help when you are responding to a crisis. They will help with customer communications and with planning for how to respond to the crisis, in general.

- How frequently do your customers purchase from you?

- What's your average transaction amount both in dollars and quantity?

- Why do your customers buy from you?

- What products and/or services do your customers buy from the competition?

- What do your customers tell their friends and family about your product and/or service?

It takes time, but you need to be obsessed with your customers. You should want to know everything about them when it comes to when, why, and how they buy what you're selling.

Throughout this chapter, we will have you obsess over every detail of your customers because we want you to find every possible way to improve and protect your business.

Why knowing your CUSTOMERS IS IMPORTANT

Most business leaders know Peter Drucker as the man who invented modern business management. One of his most famous quotes ever is, *"If you can't measure it, you can't improve it."* And when it comes to customers, you want to be able to measure everything possible.

- How loyal are your customers? Do they obsess over your products and/or services?

- How much revenue does your average customer bring in the door? Do you know what happens to your bottom line if you lose 10% of your customers? Is that 10% or 90% of your revenue? Knowing how much each customer is worth is critical to your financial projections.

- Are changes to your products and/or services needed? Are customers buying more of one product/service and moving away from a different one? Is there an opportunity to add more products? Are you wasting money producing a product that customers are no longer purchasing? Sometimes you need to sell poor performing products in order to keep your business competitive.

- Are your customers' buying habits telling you anything about the future of the market? Are customers stocking up on a certain product out of fear?

- What are your top-selling products and/or services and why? Is it the price point? Is it because it's the best value? Is it simply the best product on the market? There are a lot of reasons why a product may be your bestseller. As a business owner, you want to understand those reasons.

- Whatever it is that you sell, it's helpful to know if it fills a *want* or a *need* with your customers. Is it something they will stop purchasing when the economy is bad or when they lose their job? Or will they buy from you regardless? Is your product and/or service something that your customers purchase once and then never purchase again? How can you make yourself indispensable?

Understanding your customers provides information on how to protect your business in a crisis.

Get to know
YOUR CUSTOMERS

When it comes to knowing your customers, you have options. Here are four approaches that work well for any size business:

- **Conduct a survey**—Ask your customers specific questions about their demographics (age, income, location, etc.) and to understand why they buy your products and/or services. Best to keep the surveys short and avoid polling your customers too frequently. Once every six months is probably pushing the limit, but if you leverage the other options here, you won't need to do anything more than that. One way to increase response rates is to enter the respondents into a drawing for a gift card. People love free stuff.

- **Talk to them**—When your customers are in your store (shop, deli, gym, office, etc.) or when you have them on the phone, talk to them. Ask them how their experience has been. Ask them why they chose you over the competition. Be obsessed with them. But not in that creepy way that lands you with a restraining order—just obsessed enough to make them feel important.

- **Review their purchases**—Look at their buying history. Do they buy at regular intervals? Do they consistently buy the same products/services and is it a variety of those? How much money do they spend, on average, per purchase? What shipping method do they typically select? Do they purchase seasonally? There is so much information available with purchase history. Use it. If you are a professional service like a law firm, there's a chance that your customers only use you once when they need it. But is there something else you can assist with that your customers might not be aware of?

■ **Listen**—We know this is slightly foreign in a world where most people have their communication setting on "send" instead of "receive." So, put your communication setting to "receive" and pay attention to what your customers are saying. Read reviews. Listen to your employees while they interact with customers. Listen to yourself when you're on the phone. Listen, listen, listen. Your customers are probably more than willing to tell you what they love or hate about your product or service. Simply listen.

We recommend using as many of these approaches as possible to get to know your customers. The more you know, the easier it is to incorporate customers into your crisis planning.

Market to
YOUR CUSTOMERS

Have you paid attention to the trends from the different marketing channels? Understanding where your customers are coming from, where they are learning about your products/services, and, most importantly, how they are getting important information and updates about your business are all crucial to your marketing. Marketing is more than establishing an initial relationship. It's the ongoing interaction that builds loyalty, and this will be leveraged the most in a time of a crisis. There are some questions you should ask yourself about how you market to your customers:

■ When it comes to getting new customers or informing existing ones about new products or services, how do you do that?

- Where are your advertising dollars spent, and what is the return on those dollars?

- Are you aware of the cost of customer acquisition?

That ideal customer avatar you created earlier in the chapter can help you with marketing decisions.

If you're in crisis mode and quick decisions need to be made about how you are going to spend your time or money, marketing is something you'll need to understand. What's the fastest channel for communicating with your customer base? Which channels are the least effective? What is everyone else doing? You may want to consider doing something different, so you don't get lost in the noise. You may have to steal ideas as well. When you're in survival mode, everything is an option.

During the COVID-19 pandemic, we were all inundated with emails from businesses detailing how they were addressing safety during the pandemic. It didn't matter if you purchased something from them in 2011 or in January of 2020, and it didn't matter if what they sold was strictly digital. Every business felt the need to send out the obligatory "Here at our company; we take your safety seriously...." We would wager that for most people, this became an annoyance and background noise that they stopped paying attention to.

Corey:

During the pandemic, there were a few businesses who were able to market themselves well. One was Gaia GPS. I received an email that simply said something along the lines of "Thinking of going hiking by yourself? Download the new...."

Absolutely nowhere in the email did they mention COVID-19, a pandemic, or anything about current events. There was no need because the message about social distancing and quarantines was abundantly clear. That information was everywhere. Gaia GPS was able to connect with their audience in a way that actually made sense. Those were marketing dollars well spent.

For those other businesses who sent out those safety emails, it almost made you wonder what they were doing before the pandemic. Were their facilities not that clean to begin with? Did they not care about our safety until March of 2020?

It bears
REPEATING

All of the information in this chapter speaks to knowing your customer and why they buy from you. With so many options available, there's a reason they are spending their money with your company. What is that reason? This all goes back to your SWOT. What are those strengths that keep your customers happy?

If what you provide is critical, how do you continue to service your customers during a crisis? If you're simply a convenience, how do you stay relevant until things get better? Surviving a crisis is easier when you know your customers.

10
INTRODUCTION
TO PLANNING

> "I hated every minute of training, but I said, 'Don't quit. Suffer now and live the rest of your life as a champion.'"
> — Muhammed Ali, Boxing Champion

When it comes to creating plans, it's better to be over-prepared, never needing the plan, than to be under prepared, scrambling and caught completely by surprise when disaster strikes. We know you won't like this part because it's going to cost you the one resource you can't get more of: time. But you have to put in work if you want to survive whatever you're up against.

Muhammed Ali put the work in before the big fights so that he could win those battles at a time when it mattered most. Think of that as you build your plans. Train now so that you can win the battles later.

One of our clients owns a business in Philadelphia. She shared that she was able to leverage an existing snow emergency plan she had created as a starting point for the COVID-19 stay-at-home order. "We didn't have a plan for a global pandemic, but we had other plans in place that we could merge and use to get us through this COVID-19 crisis." The plans were sufficient enough to be quickly put into place with just a few adjustments. That's smart leadership, an efficient use of existing plans, and an easy pivot.

In **PART II: PLAN,** everything is covered that you need to know about planning. It's a comprehensive section loaded with exercises designed to prepare you for almost anything.

Grab your pen and paper. We're about to get into planning.

Why having a
PLAN IS IMPORTANT

Having some plans created that represent different types of situations (crises, events, opportunities, etc.) gives you the advantage of not having to start from zero so you can get moving quicker. The faster you respond, the faster you can focus on your business.

Having a plan could mean the difference between saving your business or closing it permanently. It could also mean you were able to capitalize on an opportunity in the market because you weren't surprised.

There's a dollar amount you can attribute to your planning. Spending time and money now will save you both in the future should a disaster strike. There have been a handful of studies on the return on investment regarding government spending on disaster preparedness. One study performed in 2018 by the National Institute of Building Sciences found that every $1 invested saved $6 when a disaster struck. While this and most other studies are based upon government spending, the concept is the same for small businesses. It also applies to your time. So, spend an hour now and save six in the future.

Corey and Julie:

One small business owner who owned and operated a machine shop in the Pacific Northwest had identified opportunities for how to ensure employees kept their jobs if orders slowed to the point where money was an issue. A few months later, when the economy started to experience a downturn, this owner was transparent with his employees about the situation, and he moved everyone to a 32-hour workweek. While the employees weren't initially thrilled with this plan, they soon realized it meant they were able to keep their jobs when many other people in the area were laid off. This business owner was able to act quickly and keep his entire team employed because he had assessed his business and already had a plan to put into place.

The takeaway: A large percentage of what you'll put into your plans will be pulled from the work you have already done.

Review your
WORK AND THINK AHEAD

Before you dive headfirst into planning, review the topics you covered that play an important role in building plans. You will use all of the work you've done so far to build plans in the current section. Gold star if you did the homework and are ready to start! Here is a bulleted list of what you'll be referencing to create some well-constructed plans:

- SWOT Analysis and Secret Sauce

- Environmental Scans

- Process Analysis

- Business Operations

- Identifying and Assessing Gaps

- Knowing Yourself

- Knowing Your People

- Knowing Your Customer

From your review of your work so far, you should now be able to identify those things that are critical to your business, whether they're processes or people. All will need to be considered when creating any plan.

Now that you have reviewed what you completed, we want to give you an idea of what we mean when we say 'crisis.' Here is a short list of examples:

- Natural disaster (earthquake, tornado, hurricane, etc.)

- Fire

- Pandemic

- Industry-specific event (supply chain issue, regulations)

- Employee specific event (strike, lottery)

- Owner specific event (unable to work, lottery)

Create a list on your own in **exercise nineteen** of what crises you may encounter. As you think through which crisis you're going to plan for first, think about the exercises you have already completed. Run through the bulleted list above one more time to make sure you're fully prepared to create your plan. Feel free to use any applicable example we've provided.

Determine the
GOAL OF THE PLAN

Plans need to have expected outcomes, or, more formally, desired future state. In some instances, your desired outcome may be that you don't lose any customers or revenue. In others, it may be that you are back up and running within a certain amount of time. It's entirely dependent upon what the crisis is and how it impacts your business, location, or industry. Nonetheless, stating objectives upfront helps you to plan better for the impacts that may come with the crisis.

In a crisis, your desired end state is likely to be "get back to normal." While this makes perfect sense, there may be an interim "end state" that needs to be planned for while you're working on your "get back to normal" plan.

As an example, if you have a plan for how to operate if your building burns down, your first goal could be getting you functional within two weeks but not at full capacity and not in your original location. Your actual end-state may be to rebuild or relocate, but there needs to be something to aim for in the meantime. You may have to outsource your work, which will eat into your margins, but you can continue at a reduced capacity servicing your most important customers. Knowing your desired end state and having a plan for how to get there *before the crisis occurs* allows you to be more prepared.

Make certain that your desired end state is attainable. If your building burns down, you don't want the goal to be "back up and running in the building within two weeks" if it isn't feasible. You have to be realistic, and our advice is to be extremely conservative with your estimations. We have learned this lesson as a direct result of working with mismanaged IT teams.

While we've never been fortunate enough to have worked with an IT team good at delivering what is promised, on time and under budget, the motto they all preach should be the goal: "under-promise and over-deliver." If you tell your customers that it will be six weeks before you open back up, and you open in four, that's a pleasant surprise; saying it will be four weeks and it turns out to be six is not. We aren't telling you to lie to your customers, but you should have a realistic public goal and an internal goal to complete ahead of schedule or under budget.

Create
ITERATIVE PLANS

We recommend that you take an iterative approach to creating these plans. It can be overwhelming to sit down and work a plan from start to finish in a single sitting.

Honestly, it's probably like writing this book. We had ambitious plans for writing the first draft in less than 30 days. That would have been nearly impossible. There are chapters that we spent days writing. Not a single day, but days. And then we rewrote them. And rewrote them again. The order and content matter, and how we convey both is important. Creating a crisis plan is no different.

All of the details matter. The immediate steps could define how everything else is handled, so getting the plan right is critical. Spend time on it. Work through it in chunks. Determine what is critical for the plan to be successful. Then, think about what tasks will need to occur. Think about the other things that aren't important—the "nice to haves" versus the "need to haves."

You will probably have to make some tough decisions about what things aren't necessary. Once you feel confident in those steps, decide on which tool to use, what your milestones are, and how you'll collaborate with your team on creating the plans. Now you're ready to create the plan.

Use the Create-Review-Update approach. Create a section, then put it away or send it to someone else to review. If you're doing your own reviews, pick it back up later and review it. Does it make sense? Is anything missing? Are there items listed that don't need to be included? Make the updates and then start the next section. Building a plan is time-consuming, but it doesn't have to be overwhelming.

Keep in mind that the plans don't have to be perfect. Evolve them as you gain more knowledge and as you become stronger at planning. Much like growing into a strong leader, you need to grow your planning muscle. It's not a skill that everyone is born with, so give yourself grace as you become a better planner over time.

Also, know that you may have some gaps in your plan until you need to execute it. This is to be expected. You can't possibly plan for everything, and your plan needs to be flexible enough to be used somewhere else. Expect blind spots, and accept them as part of the process.

Having plans in place allows for the possibility to make improvements and advances before a crisis even happens. You have done the hard work with all of the assessments and planning. Put that information to use to make your business bulletproof.

Pull it
ALL TOGETHER

When you're building plans, build them in a manner that makes the most sense for you and your business. There are a lot of options for how to craft plans, and the most important part of any plan is usability. So, as you start to lay out the plan, use an approach and tool that makes it easy (we review tools in **CHAPTER 12: CREATE THE PLAN**). There's freedom within the framework.

And if you need help, ask. It's okay to be unsure of how to do this. For most people, this type of planning is new. You're going to have questions, so ask them. Ask your leadership team. Ask a business mentor. Ask for outside help. Ask us! You don't want to find out the hard way that you have a major gap in your plan.

Julie:

More than once in my career I've had to create a plan for something I didn't understand. Let me be clear—it's not because I'm unintelligent or because I wasn't paying attention. It's because leadership didn't clearly define the desired end state and hadn't identified what was important for the project.

Now, I can plan for anything. Do you want to physically move your business across the country while simultaneously launching a new product? I've got you covered. Do you need to integrate three companies while moving all of them to a new computer system? I'm your girl. But you know what I can't do? Read your mind.

While I can give you recommendations based upon my knowledge and professional experience, I can't tell you what your desired end state is, and I can't tell you what's important to the project versus what's nice to have. That's on you as the leader.

If you want to build a successful plan, you have to know where you're going. It's that simple.

Your plan's
LEVEL OF DETAIL

If you're the type of person who gets excited about creating a plan, welcome to Julie's world. She loves a good plan. Lots of details. Every possible scenario covered. Throw in all the necessary predecessors and successors and...well, it's the stuff dreams are made of—for a planner. But if you're not a planner, or if the thought of creating a plan sends you into a panic, have no fear; you're not alone.

Can Others
PERFORM IT?

In most instances, the only person who truly needs to use the plan is you. Would it benefit your business during a crisis if others on your team could pick up the plan and execute it? Of course! Is it necessary? Not really. Consider the possibility that the crisis might be that you can't perform your role anymore.

Assume you are stuck in Greece on an extended family vacation, and there's no definitive timeline for when you can return. It could happen. It did for one of our clients. The point is, if you want to create a plan that only you can understand and execute, that's okay. But if others can also understand it, bonus!

Both
STRAIGHTFORWARD AND COMPLEX

Do what's best for your business, employees, and customers. Certain parts may have to be more detailed than others, depending on the complexity. Some parts could be very simple if the tasks are straightforward. In our warehouse freezer sprinkler example, it could have been as simple as having directions such as "Go to the utility room outside of maintenance and turn the main sprinkler valve in the center of the wall to 'off.'" Keep them as simple as possible while remaining functional.

However, other areas of the plan will require complexity. Consider the law of requisite variety: this is a fancy term for ensuring your solutions (and the people executing the plan) appropriately match the problems.

Recycle, Reuse,
RENEW

The first plan you create will be the toughest because you're most likely starting from scratch. But each subsequent plan will become easier because you'll be able to reuse parts and pieces. You aren't creating plans that are 100% unique, which will make the process faster once you get going.

Start your
FIRST PLAN

Look back at the list of scenarios you brainstormed earlier in the chapter. Pick one to use for your plan creation throughout the rest of **PART II: PLAN.** If you have some other, more specific worst-case scenario, feel free to use that.

For all of the exercises in the upcoming chapters, we will use a generic plan for a product recall to help demonstrate how to build this plan. While that's not a major event like a natural disaster, we're using the example to help demonstrate different ideas and how to approach them.

As we mentioned before, we use the terms disaster, crisis, and problem interchangeably. Though you will likely think about major disasters when crisis planning is mentioned, you should also think about those things that may be minor but could cause major problems: say, a water leak from your upstairs neighbor which causes mold damage and a shutdown of your business. Yes, that's very specific, but that's how we want you to think.

Tips for
SOLOPRENEURS

For all the solopreneurs out there, it's a blessing and a curse—you get to do this work on your own (unless you hire someone to build the plans). This means you have complete control over how detailed the plans are, what the desired end state is, and what's important to include in each plan.

As you create plans, you should strongly consider leveraging someone in your network to complete a review. Overall, you're doing this work on your own.

11 THE STRUCTURE OF A PLAN

> "Make everything as simple as possible, but not simpler."
> — Albert Einstein, Theoretical Physicist

What should the
PLAN INCLUDE?

When you're building the plan, you get to decide how detailed it needs to be. As we discussed in **CHAPTER 10: INTRODUCTION TO PLANNING,** as long as someone can access the plan and execute it, it has enough detail. If someone else on your team is writing the plan, trust but verify. You don't want to discover you can't execute the plan because you didn't participate in a review.

At the beginning of **CHAPTER 1: THE FOUNDATION,** we mentioned a client Julie had who was living proof of Murphy's Law: exploding sewer pipes, dead animals in the ceiling, employee drug ring busts, and ice skating rinks in the freezer. Well, there's more.

Julie:

We had another "event" occur where we were moving them to a new computer system. This is a very detailed and very long process starting on Friday; it involves migrating data and performing essentially every task they have to ensure they can still do business when they reopen on Monday. It's the culmination of months of planning, preparation, training, and hard work.

The cut-over started at 4:00 AM on a Friday. There were a couple of hiccups along the way but nothing major. Still, it was enough to slow us down by a few hours. We were hoping to be done with the systematic portion of the weekend by 11:00 PM on Friday. We went long by five hours, finishing at 4:00 AM Saturday.

I crawled in bed around 4:30 AM.

At 7:45 AM, my phone rang. I answered, but I don't think I was awake.

Me: *Hello.*

Vice President of Human Resources: *Oh—did I wake you?*

Me: *No.* (Apparently, I'm a liar when I'm asleep.)

VP: *I wanted to let you know that the fire trucks and police are on the scene and everything will be okay.*

Me: [JOLTS AWAKE] *Did you say "firetrucks and police"?*

VP: *Yeah. But it's fine. Go back to sleep.* (Apparently, I'm not a *good* liar when I'm asleep.)

click

When I arrived at the client site 20 minutes later, there were, as expected, fire trucks and police cars everywhere. Shortly after 4:00 AM, a drunk driver had hit the main transformer across the street from the warehouse and blew the power for the entire block. No big deal—the warehouse backup generators were there to kick on in case of a power loss. But, there was no plan in place to regularly check the generators, and they weren't working. Murphy's Law.

Structure
THE PLAN

While you could structure a plan in numerous ways, we build our plans so they are organized by the start date. It's unlikely you'll be creating your plans in a tool that allows for easy expanding and collapsing, so make sure that tasks are easy to find on a daily (or sometimes hourly) basis.

Wherever possible, every task should have a resource/person assigned, a duration (how long will the task take), and predecessors and successors linking them all together (things that have to happen before or after a task). Here is a sample layout for an example scenario we made up for a product recall:

#	Traits	Title	Given Earliest Start	Expected Start	Expected End	Planned Duration	Resources	Predecessors	Successors
0	▼	Recall Disaster Plan III	Oct 7	Oct 7	Nov 17	1.5m?	External Resource; Recall...		
1		▼ Phase I - Immediate Action		Oct 7	Oct 10	3.25 days	External Resource; Recall...		
2		▼ Begin Initial Response		Oct 7	Oct 10	3.25 days	External Resource; Recall...		
3		▷ Notification From Supplier Of Recall		Oct 7	Oct 7	1 hour	External Resource		4
4		▷ Communicate Recall To Leadership		Oct 7	Oct 7	1 hour	Recall Manager	3	5
5		▷ Check POs For Affected Time		Oct 7	Oct 7	2 hours	Recall Manager	4	6; 7
6		▷ IF NO PROD RECEIVED PLAN ENDS		Oct 7	Oct 7	1 hour	Recall Manager	5	12; 13
7		▷ Respond To Vendor That We Have Prod		Oct 7	Oct 7	1 hour	Recall Manager	5	8
8		▷ Communicate To Inventory Control		Oct 7	Oct 7	1 hour	Recall Manager	7	9
9		▷ Pull Invoices		Oct 7	Oct 8	4 hours	Recall Manager	8	10
10		▷ Locate & Pull Product From Warehouse		Oct 8	Oct 8	4 hours	Inventory Control	9	11
11		▷ Send Comms To Recall Person Product Is Pulled		Oct 8	Oct 8	1 hour	Inventory Control	10	12
12		▷ Communicate Status To Leadership		Oct 8	Oct 8	1 hour	Recall Manager	6; 11	13
13		▷ Communicate Recall Info & Status To Sales		Oct 9	Oct 9	1 hour	Recall Manager	6; 12	14
14		Initial Internal Response Complete		Oct 9	Oct 9			13	15
15		▷ Determine If Product Out For Delivery		Oct 9	Oct 9	1 hour	Recall Manager; Inventory...	14	16; 17
16		▷ IF YES, NOTIFY DRIVERS		Oct 9	Oct 9	2 hours	Transportation	15	18
17		▷ IF NO, ID CUSTOMERS & SHIPMENT		Oct 9	Oct 9	4 hours	Customer Service Rep	15	19; 22
18		▷ Note & Pull From Truck		Oct 9	Oct 10	6 hours	Driver	16	19
19		In-Transit Response Complete		Oct 10	Oct 10			17; 18	

Your plan may be easier to follow if you break it into phases. Here is what we have used for our sample plan that we will be referencing throughout this section.

- **Phase I**: Immediate Action

- **Phase II:** Next Steps

- **Phase III:** Maintain During Crisis

- **Phase IV**: Return to Normal

We know it can be challenging to get all of the information we recommend for each task, but at a minimum, you'll want to identify what resources are needed for everything listed in the plan. This is especially true for Phase I, as that's the time when things will be the most chaotic and you'll be making decisions quickly.

Communication
TASKS

From this point forward, you're going to hear us consistently talk about communication. The reality is, most organizations struggle in this area even when they aren't in crisis mode. Keeping your people informed, being transparent, and answering tough questions is part of leadership, and in a crisis, you'll need to be strong. You should be the type of leader who understands the importance of communication, so start reinforcing that behavior. Our recommendation (STRONG RECOMMENDATION) is that you add tasks specific to communications. At a minimum, here is who should be considered when building these tasks:

- Employees

- Customers

- Suppliers

- Support Team (accountants, lawyers, etc.)

We understand that communicating when things are confusing is tough, but there is a way to do so that keeps folks calm, builds trust, and stops (or dramatically slows) rumors. If there's one thing we have witnessed again and again in every company, it's that people will make things up in the absence of information.

Don't give people a reason to fabricate information. Communicate.

Supporting
INFORMATION

Before you go too much deeper into plan creation, spend a little more time on supporting information.

Supporting information is anything you'll need quick access to in a crisis and don't want to have to spend time searching for. This could include things like:

- Emergency services (911 is obvious, but specific numbers may be needed)
- Government resources (inspectors, etc.)
- Utilities (contact info, account numbers)
- Employee contact information
- Attorney and accountant phone numbers
- Copies of insurance policies
- Financial information
- Benefits information (health insurance policies)
- Vendor contact information

You'll want to have this information available both printed and electronically. Create a one-page document that has critical information that can be easily accessed. You want to do everything possible to minimize the chaos when you're executing one of these plans. Be prepared.

What you can
LIVE WITHOUT

Julie:

When I was a kid, I watched reruns of *Gilligan's Island*. First, why couldn't they ever get off that island? They made a radio out of a coconut shell! How did that intelligence not translate into finding a way home? Second, why did Mrs. Howell pack enough clothes for a 3-month vacation when they were embarking on a 3-hour tour?

You may be saying to yourself, "Well, she used everything she brought." And she did, but almost everyone else got along fine with the same outfit every day. Take only what's necessary. Think lean. You'll be in crisis mode. It may not be obvious now, but you'll want fast and simple when you're in the actual crisis. So, don't add extra work that doesn't need to be there. Don't be a Lovey Howell.

 Grab your workbook and turn to **exercise twenty**. You'll see we listed out things we could live without based on our recall crisis. We included a sample here as well:

LIVE WITHOUT:

- Formalized role for recall resources
- Allocated budget for recall plan
- Building end-to-end processes for every potential recall scenario
- Plan that includes every possible step—high level is fine
- Formalized internal communication plan
- Certain customers may get service interrupted
- May need to cut promos/sales to reduce demand

While you're creating your plan, you'll want to keep that list close as you add your milestones and tasks because you may find that something you've placed on the *Live Without* list may need to be a part of the crisis plan you are building. In **PART III: EXECUTE,** we address how it is fairly common to have tasks that won't be executed. This could be for several different reasons. Perhaps the crisis isn't as severe as you predicted. Maybe the task isn't as critical as you initially estimated, so you could skip that task. Here's an easy example: You have customer communications in your disaster plan. After the crisis has happened, you've reviewed everything, you've realized there will be no impact to your customers, and, therefore, you cut customer communications out of your plan. It's not unusual to learn more about the plan and how to execute it as you move through the process.

By this point in the process, you should have a good idea of what tasks to include and what types to exclude. When you're building your plans, take time to review each task, asking yourself if it's a "need to have" or "nice to have."

12 CREATE THE PLAN

"If I had nine hours to chop down a tree, I'd spend the first six sharpening my axe."
— Abraham Lincoln, 16th President of the United States

We had the pleasure of talking with Harry Boyd, Emergency Management Coordinator at the Virginia Museum of Fine Arts (VMFA), during the COVID-19 pandemic. His department is responsible for preparing for any disaster or emergency that could occur. Aside from giving us advice on everything from who should be involved (everyone) to what to plan for (get as obscure as possible—it will likely happen), he said the best advice for a small business is to talk to as many people as possible and network wherever you can. You should also reach out to local law enforcement and other emergency services when applicable as they "would much rather help prevent an emergency than respond to one."

On a side note for all of those out there who were affected by the 2020 pandemic: Don't feel bad. Even the VMFA didn't have a pandemic plan in their playbook, but they did have other plans that they applied to that crisis.

So we have covered why plans are important and how all of the work completed so far is going to make building plans easier. We have also looked at what plans should include and what is unnecessary. Now it's time to start creating.

Should you include
YOUR TEAM?

Whether you include your team in building out the plans or you create them alone is a personal decision. If you have a strong team and believe they would add value to the process, then include the team. Maybe you're fortunate enough that the entirety of this project could be assigned to someone in the organization.

Like we noted in **CHAPTER 8: KNOW YOUR PEOPLE**, you should find out what everyone's professional background is and if they have some sort of emergency management experience. This was something we picked up directly from Harry. His suggestion was to find out if anyone on your team has a law enforcement, emergency medical services, or military background because they likely already have emergency response training. You may be able to leverage their knowledge and training and even assign them to be your crisis manager.

It truly doesn't matter who creates the plans; they just need to be created.

Tool
SELECTION

When it comes to what tool to use, you have options. Here is a partial list of tools we've used for you to consider along with some quick thoughts on each:

TOOL OPTION	PROS	CONS
Microsoft Project	• Feature-rich • Designed for managing projects • Robust reporting options • Provides budgeting within the tool	• Expensive • Significant learning curve
Pen and Paper	• Readily available • Easy to use • Great for checklists • Good for started a branstorm	• Risk of misplacing • No reporting • Hard to organize tasks
Microsoft Excel	• Easy task separation (rows/columns) • Create charts and graphs to show progress • Can sort tasks • Moderate to easy to use	• Not designed for project plans • Dependencies & Successors hard to manage • Reporting minimal
Google Sheets	• Easy to use • Collaborative • Free • Create charts and graphs to show progress • Easy task separation (rows/columns) • Can sort tasks	• Not designed for project plans • Reporting minimal
Merlin Project	• Designed for creating project plans • Not free, but reasonably priced • Collaborative • Easy to use • Reporting options	• Not as feature-rich as Microsoft Project • Not free, but reasonably priced • Not great for complicated project plans

For the purposes of this book, we are going to create our plans using Merlin Project. We selected this tool because it's inexpensive, collaborative, and offers features that make managing a project easier.

You'll note that under Merlin Project, we have listed "Not free, but reasonably priced" as both a pro and a con. The reason we took this approach is that there are many free options available. To some, having to pay a fee would be negative. But the fact that it's reasonably priced is a pro, especially since the tool is designed for managing projects, and it's nowhere near the cost of Microsoft Project.

Most online tools have a free trial period you can use to evaluate their product. Try them out, and don't overthink it. Use what is most comfortable for your business. No matter what you choose, a tool selection should be made now before moving forward with creating a plan. Set yourself up for success.

Identify
MILESTONES

By this point, you have settled on a tool and you have picked the first crisis to plan for. Start identifying milestones.

The easiest way to define a milestone is this: Milestones mark key events in a project. They are signposts within your project, guiding you from start to finish. Milestones don't impact the duration of a project; in fact, milestones don't have durations (which we cover later) assigned. We will work through some examples to give you a better idea of how to get started.

Continuing with the product recall as the example scenario, the milestones could be:

- Initial Internal Response Complete
- In-Transit Response Complete
- ID Impacted Customers Complete
- Pick-up Product Complete
- Customer Communication Complete
- Cost Recovery Complete

In **CHAPTER 13: BUILD AND EXPAND YOUR PLAN**, you'll add tasks to each of the milestones, but for now, this is all the work needed.

 Open your workbook to the instructions for **exercise twenty-one** and start listing your milestones on the plan page. Eventually, you will be creating plans in the tool you selected, but as you work through the learning curve and pull all the pieces of plan creation together, we suggest you do the exercises in the workbook. We've designed the workbook to teach you how to increase the quality of the plan you're building incrementally. Once you have created a plan using the workbook, your transition to using a project management tool will be much smoother.

Here are what our milestones look like in our recall plan and what you should take away:

Traits	Title	Given Earliest Start	Expected Start	Expected End
▣ ⊘	▼ **Recall Disaster Plan Milestones**	Oct 7, 2025	Oct 7	Nov 17
	Phase IV - Return to Normal		Oct 7	Oct 7
	In-Transit Response Complete		Oct 10	Oct 10
	ID Affected Customers Complete		Oct 7	Oct 7
	Pick-up Product Complete		Oct 23	Oct 23
	Customer Communication Complete		Oct 30	Oct 30
	Cost Recovery Complete		Nov 17	Nov 17
	Resume normal operations		Nov 17	Nov 17

- Milestone name

- Duration for milestones is always 0

As we start to build more tasks and details into the example plan, the dates of the milestone— planned start date and finish date—will change based on the supporting tasks. If you're using a planning program such as Microsoft Project and have it set up correctly, the dates will update automatically, which is a bonus of using a project planning tool. (This feature isn't available if you aren't using a project planning tool.)

Tips for
SOLOPRENEURS

Technically, there's nothing you would do differently to create a plan. However, as a solopreneur, you could easily take advantage of creating your plans in a tool that isn't necessarily made for project management, such as Google Sheets or Excel. As the management and execution of the plan will be completed 100% by you, you're the only one who needs to know what's happening.

Of course, you can still go the route of using a tool that's built for managing projects, but it would be quite easy to get away with something very simple.

13 BUILD AND EXPAND YOUR PLAN

"When we strive to become better than we are, everything around us becomes better too."
— Paulo Coelho, Author

Julie:

Early in my career, I had a boss who was a project management wizard. To this day, Earl still tops my list of bosses who taught me valuable career lessons. He taught me how to build great project plans that are easy to execute against, which is truly the most important element of a plan. What value would a project plan have if you can't successfully execute the tasks? I don't know a single person who uses printed out project schedules to decorate their home or office, so I shouldn't worry if they aren't pretty? They need to be functional.

The first plan I created for Earl sucked. It sucked bad. And I didn't even know it sucked until I sat down and reviewed it with Earl. During the review, he was careful not to demoralize me with his feedback, but rather coached me through small incremental changes I could make to improve the overall plan. Over several months, my plans improved dramatically.

That's one of the great things about project plans: you create the baseline plan and then add in additional tasks and detail as you iterate through. Unless you're a clairvoyant, your plan isn't going to be perfect. We've never had a situation where a plan didn't need adjusting as it was executed regardless of how many hours we spent creating the plan. Surprises happen.

Create
A PLAN

By this point, you should be familiar with what you'll leverage to create a plan, so it's time to dig a little deeper. In **CHAPTER 11: THE STRUCTURE OF A PLAN,** we recommended building a plan that was based on phases. You can revisit that if you need a refresher on what they were or view them on the following image.

Throughout this chapter, we will carefully explain plan creation. Remember, the approach we are taking is to create one plan initially and then copy information from that plan to the next because there will certainly be duplication—we encourage it! Here is how we are breaking this down into bite-size pieces:

- Identify what tasks need to be included for each milestone

- Determine durations and link tasks

- Identify resources

- Identify and plan for constraints

- Create your communication plan

Start by assigning your milestones to the phases you've created. If you have a milestone that you believe happens in two phases, then list it in both for now. Either you'll get clarification later as you add tasks, or you'll leave it listed twice. You can have something listed more than once, especially if it's important to your business.

 You can complete this in your workbook by heading back to **exercise twenty-one**.

Here is an example of a plan with phases and the corresponding milestones:

# ▲	Traits	Title	Given Earliest Start	Expected Start	Expected End
0	▪⊘	▼ Recall Disaster Plan Milestones	Oct 7	Oct 7	Nov 17
1		▼ Phase I - Immediate Action		Oct 7	Oct 10
2		▶ Begin Initial Response		Oct 7	Oct 10
19		In-Transit Response Complete		Oct 10	Oct 10
20		▼ Phase II - Next Steps		Oct 7	Oct 30
21		▶ Begin ID Affected Customers		Oct 9	Oct 10
25		ID Affected Customers Complete		Oct 7	Oct 7
26		▶ Begin Pick-up Product		Oct 10	Oct 23
33		Pick-up Product Complete		Oct 23	Oct 23
34		▶ Begin Customer Communications		Oct 22	Oct 30
39		Customer Communication Complete		Oct 30	Oct 30
40		▼ Phase III - Maintain During Crisis		Oct 30	Nov 17
41		▶ Begin Cost Recovery		Oct 30	Nov 17
46		Cost Recovery Complete		Nov 17	Nov 17
47		▼ Phase IV - Return to Normal		Nov 17	Nov 17
48		Resume normal operations		Nov 17	Nov 17

Identify
TASKS

With your milestones identified and bucketed by phase, the next step is to identify all tasks that need to be done for your plan.

A task is defined as a single unit of work or a single step in a multi-step plan. The easiest way to get a comprehensive list of tasks is by looking back at the exercises you have completed throughout the book. The output from each exercise can be used to create a comprehensive task list.

Here are the exercises you have completed and should review for task creation:

- **Review your SWOT**—Carefully review the strengths section to identify any impacts. For example, if you have strengths related to customer service or product quality, include tasks in your plan that address these areas. You want to protect your strengths as they are critical to your business's success. (Hint: In this case, protecting your strength means transparent communications and an action plan to assist impacted customers.) Revisit any Threats and Weaknesses identified in the SWOT analysis that have not been addressed yet; review these and add a task if it's applicable to this particular crisis.

- **Review your environmental scans**—Determine if there are any threats or opportunities that apply. The plan you're creating may be a direct result of a scan.

- **Revisit your business process review**—At the very least, be sure to include all critical process that may be affected.

- **Preserve your secret sauce**—You should always be working to preserve your secret sauce.

- **Know your financials**—Be aware of your financials and the impact they will have on your plan. This includes knowing who you can contact for additional cash flow, what your financial safety net looks like, and how to perform a high-level ROI when needed.

- **Consider your exit strategies**—Know what your thresholds are for exiting the business. Your exit strategy may not necessarily be a task in the plan; it may simply be a reminder to yourself of the conditions in which you would exit. You did some work on the exit strategy. Carefully consider that information as well.

- **Review your gaps**—You identified gaps that you should consider during crisis planning. A gap you identified may even be the point of your plan.

- **Know your people**—You'll want to consider everything you learned about yourself, your people, and your customers. What are your personal strengths and weaknesses as a leader? Who does everyone lean on in your team when times get tough? How loyal are your customers and to what products/services? The things you learned in this section of the book may or may not be milestones or tasks in the plan, but they need to be considered.

As you reviewed the exercises you completed, did you identify any additional milestones? If yes, add them to the corresponding phase.

Now, for each milestone, identify tasks that need to occur for that milestone to happen. For the recall example, we will use "Initial Internal Response Complete" as the milestone around which we build tasks.

As you list out each task that is required to reach a milestone, it's helpful to keep some key questions in mind:

- How long will it take me to complete this task? If you don't know the duration, create an estimate or set a reasonable expectation.

- When does this task need to be completed? If you know the time/date, great. If not, you should at least know the order it goes in.

- Who will complete this task?

- Will any additional components be needed to complete this task? (Internet service, phone numbers, outside resources, etc.)

- Does this task have to be performed at a specific physical location?

Now that we have walked through an example, it's time to start identifying tasks.

 We left space in the workbook to complete this (**exercise twenty-two**).

# ▲	Traits	Title	Given Earliest Start	Expected Start	Expected End
0	🗂⊘	▼ Recall Disaster Plan III	Oct 7	Oct 7	Nov 17
1		▼ Phase I - Immediate Action		Oct 7	Oct 10
2		▼ Begin Initial Response		Oct 7	Oct 10
3		▷ Notification From Supplier Of Recall		Oct 7	Oct 7
4		▷ Communicate Recall To Leadership		Oct 7	Oct 7
5		▷ Check POs For Affected Time		Oct 7	Oct 7
6		▷ IF NO PROD RECEIVED PLAN ENDS		Oct 7	Oct 7
7		▷ Respond To Vendor That We Have Prod		Oct 7	Oct 7
8		▷ Communicate To Inventory Control		Oct 7	Oct 7
9		▷ Pull Invoices		Oct 7	Oct 8
10		▷ Locate & Pull Product From Warehouse		Oct 8	Oct 8
11		▷ Send Comms To Recall Person Product Is Pulled		Oct 8	Oct 8
12		▷ Communicate Status To Leadership		Oct 8	Oct 8
13		▷ Communicate Recall Info & Status To Sales		Oct 9	Oct 9
14		Initial Internal Response Complete		Oct 9	Oct 9
15		▷ Determine If Product Out For Delivery		Oct 9	Oct 9
16		▷ IF YES, NOTIFY DRIVERS		Oct 9	Oct 9
17		▷ IF NO, ID CUSTOMERS & SHIPMENT		Oct 9	Oct 9
18		▷ Note & Pull From Truck		Oct 9	Oct 10
19		In-Transit Response Complete		Oct 10	Oct 10

Our phase is listed on row 1, and the supporting tasks to complete the milestone (row 19) are listed in rows 3-18.

Add durations
AND LINK TASKS

If you have ever created task-oriented plans in the past, you know they are typically based on timelines. Even if you're creating a task list for the week (or just the day), the list is based on completing tasks in a certain amount of time. With crisis plans, there will be tasks that have to be completed, and until you're executing the plan, you won't know what the timeline is. The amount of time you *need* to complete a task may have to be compressed due to urgency. The same is true for the amount of time you *have* to complete a task. Keep in mind that if you normally don't have time constraints around tasks that are performed, you might when a crisis happens.

When you're creating the plan, base the timeline on best guesses. You know your business well, so you should know how long tasks will take to complete. Unfortunately, unless you have been through this crisis before, it's hard to know how much time you will need to execute.

#	Traits	Title	Given Earliest Start	Planned Duration	Expected Start	Expected End	Predecessors	Successors
0	■⊘	▼ Recall Disaster Plan III	Oct 7	1.46 months	Oct 7	Nov 17		
1		▼ Phase I - Immediate Action		3.25 days	Oct 7	Oct 10		
2		▼ Begin Initial Response		3.25 days	Oct 7	Oct 10		
3		▷ Notification From Supplier Of Recall		1 hour	Oct 7	Oct 7		4
4		▷ Communicate Recall To Leadership		1 hour	Oct 7	Oct 7	3	5
5		▷ Check POs For Affected Time		2 hours	Oct 7	Oct 7	4	6; 7
6		▷ IF NO PROD RECEIVED PLAN ENDS		1 hour	Oct 7	Oct 7	5	12; 13
7		▷ Respond To Vendor That We Have Prod		1 hour	Oct 7	Oct 7	5	8
8		▷ Communicate To Inventory Control		1 hour	Oct 7	Oct 7	7	9
9		▷ Pull Invoices		4 hours	Oct 8	Oct 8	8	10
10		▷ Locate & Pull Product From Warehouse		4 hours	Oct 8	Oct 8	9	11
11		▷ Send Comms To Recall Person Product Is Pulled		1 hour	Oct 8	Oct 8	10	12
12		▷ Communicate Status To Leadership		1 hour	Oct 8	Oct 8	6; 11	13
13		▷ Communicate Recall Info & Status To Sales		1 hour	Oct 9	Oct 9	6; 12	14
14		Initial Internal Response Complete			Oct 9	Oct 9	13	15
15		▷ Determine If Product Out For Delivery		1 hour	Oct 9	Oct 9	14	16; 17
16		▷ IF YES, NOTIFY DRIVERS		2 hours	Oct 9	Oct 9	15	18
17		▷ IF NO, ID CUSTOMERS & SHIPMENT		4 hours	Oct 9	Oct 9	15	19; 22
18		▷ Note & Pull From Truck		6 hours	Oct 10	Oct 10	16	19
19		In-Transit Response Complete			Oct 10	Oct 10	17; 18	

As you can see in the above image, we added durations into our recall plan.

The best way to determine the duration is to ask the people who would most likely be completing the work. Even if they can provide an educated answer, you may have to make some estimations for some of the tasks. We recommend that you estimate high, as you want to leave yourself enough time to complete the work. It's also not a problem if the durations you give aren't exact because you can leverage linking your tasks with your predecessors and successors to help control when tasks begin. That will be covered shortly.

As there are so many unknowns with execution, be as thorough as possible when you're building the plan. Set aside time to work on the plan and consider every detail of your business. It's more important to be thorough than it is to be fast. For each task you have listed, put an estimate of how long it will take to complete.

In addition to durations, you'll want to create some type of schedule to indicate when a task should be started (and also completed).

One simple approach for indicating when a task should start is to use the +X method, where X is the number of days from when the crisis started (or when some other task was completed). This logic is commonly referred to as linking or working with predecessors and successors in project management terms.

- Contact vendors +1 day. In this instance, we would contact our vendors one day after the crisis has started.

- Contact vendors +2 days after the bank was contacted. In this instance, we wouldn't contact our vendors until 2 days after we have spoken to the bank.

For every task listed in the plan, you will need to identify both the duration and when the task should start. As this plan is dealing with a crisis, there will likely be a large number of tasks that need to be completed within the first 48 to 72 hours of kicking off the plan.

Review each task identified and enter a duration and a start date. This is possible to do if you're planning on doing something like a product launch, but it's not always possible to plan for when a crisis would hit, so utilize a "Day 0" as the start date to be filled in later.

 Head over to **exercise twenty-three** to fill out your durations.

If you're using a project management tool that is specifically designed for creating projects, such as Microsoft Project, then entering start dates will be significantly easier because you can use the predecessor/successor (linked from/linked to) feature. In the example below, you'll see the two rightmost columns labeled "Predecessors" and "Successors." This is where tasks are linked together to control when a task starts. Here are two examples to further explain task linking.

Task 6—IF NO PROD RECEIVED PLAN ENDS cannot start until task 5 is complete, which is *Check POs For Affected Time*. Once task 6 is complete, then tasks 12 and 13 can begin. You can see how both tasks 12 and 13 are linked to task 6.

Task 11—Send Comms To Recall Person Product Is Pulled cannot start until task 10 completes. Task 10 is *Locate & Pull Product from Warehouse*. Once task 11 completes, task 12 can begin.

#	Traits	Title	Given Earliest Start	Planned Duration	Expected Start	Expected End	Predecessors	Successors
0	▣⏱	▼ Recall Disaster Plan III	Oct 7	1.46 months	Oct 7	Nov 17		
1		▼ Phase I - Immediate Action		3.25 days	Oct 7	Oct 10		
2		▼ Begin Initial Response		3.25 days	Oct 7	Oct 10		
3		▷ Notification From Supplier Of Recall		1 hour	Oct 7	Oct 7		4
4		▷ Communicate Recall To Leadership		1 hour	Oct 7	Oct 7	3	5
5		▷ Check POs For Affected Time		2 hours	Oct 7	Oct 7	4	6; 7
6		▷ IF NO PROD RECEIVED PLAN ENDS		1 hour	Oct 7	Oct 7	5	12; 13
7		▷ Respond To Vendor That We Have Prod		1 hour	Oct 7	Oct 7	5	8
8		▷ Communicate To Inventory Control		1 hour	Oct 7	Oct 7	7	9
9		▷ Pull Invoices		4 hours	Oct 8	Oct 8	8	10
10		▷ Locate & Pull Product From Warehouse		4 hours	Oct 8	Oct 8	9	11
11		▷ Send Comms To Recall Person Product Is Pulled		1 hour	Oct 8	Oct 8	10	12
12		▷ Communicate Status To Leadership		1 hour	Oct 8	Oct 8	6; 11	13
13		▷ Communicate Recall Info & Status To Sales		1 hour	Oct 9	Oct 9	6; 12	14
14		Initial Internal Response Complete			Oct 9	Oct 9	13	15
15		▷ Determine If Product Out For Delivery		1 hour	Oct 9	Oct 9	14	16; 17
16		▷ IF YES, NOTIFY DRIVERS		2 hours	Oct 9	Oct 9	15	18
17		▷ IF NO, ID CUSTOMERS & SHIPMENT		4 hours	Oct 9	Oct 9	15	19; 22
18		▷ Note & Pull From Truck		6 hours	Oct 10	Oct 10	16	19
19		In-Transit Response Complete			Oct 10	Oct 10	17; 18	

Linking tasks together is the most effective approach to controlling start dates and times and results in a well-constructed timeline for your plan. However, this functionality is very specific to a project management software. If your selected tool isn't designed specifically to create and manage project plans, you won't have this feature available to you.

Regardless of what tool you are using, this part can get confusing. Take your time.

You can work on linking tasks in the workbook (using **exercise twenty-three again**). If you have questions along the way, it may be helpful to review the sample layout that's in your workbook. There's an example project to view in the "Examples" workbook to help you create your plan.

Identify
RESOURCES

Every comprehensive plan created includes resources. This extends beyond people to include places and things.

Task ownership addresses the people part of resource planning. As we said in **CHAPTER 10: INTRODUCTION TO PLANNING**, you'll want to assign ownership of tasks to people, but because you're creating plans for something that may not happen for years (or ideally, *never* happens) you should use the practice of assigning tasks by role within the organization rather than by name. The single biggest benefit to this approach is that you don't have to update a plan every time someone leaves or joins the organization.

As you are creating the plans, keep in mind you may need to run on a leaner staff, especially if there is no revenue coming in— so this means fewer people to complete the tasks. If someone is mission-critical, use their role as a task owner, but if they aren't, avoid listing them. You can always update roles later, depending on who is available when the crisis occurs. Adjust once more information is available.

Something to note as you create your plans: Just because someone fills a particular role today doesn't necessarily mean they are the person who should do that work during a crisis.

Corey and Julie:

One of our clients was having system issues, and for some reason, over 80% of their customers received surcharges on their invoices for no logical reason. The client needed all hands on deck to contact the customers and personally let them know that they were aware of the issue and working on it. The customer service manager, who should have been running damage control in customer service, wasn't able to focus completely on the problem because she was also significantly involved with working on the solution with the IT department. We suggested to the client that they bring in their sales managers to help direct traffic in customer service until the problem was resolved. If there is someone else who can execute tasks, leverage those people.

You may also need to identify places or things in your plan; list these as additional resources. As an example, planning for a natural disaster may require you to identify temporary locations to work from or resources to use, like online collaboration tools. All resources should be listed in the plan.

 Complete this in your workbook, using **exercise twenty-four**

Here's what the recall plan looks like with resources added:

#	Traits	Title	Given Earliest Start	Expected Start	Expected End	Planned Duration	Resources	Predecessors	Successors
0	📁🕐	▼ Recall Disaster Plan III	Oct 7	Oct 7	Nov 17	1.5m?	External Resource; Recall...		
1		▼ Phase I - Immediate Action		Oct 7	Oct 10	3.25 days	External Resource; Recall...		
2		▼ Begin Initial Response		Oct 7	Oct 10	3.25 days	External Resource; Recall...		
3		▷ Notification From Supplier Of Recall		Oct 7	Oct 7	1 hour	External Resource		4
4		▷ Communicate Recall To Leadership		Oct 7	Oct 7	1 hour	Recall Manager	3	5
5		▷ Check POs For Affected Time		Oct 7	Oct 7	2 hours	Recall Manager	4	6; 7
6		▷ IF NO PROD RECEIVED PLAN ENDS		Oct 7	Oct 7	1 hour	Recall Manager	5	12; 13
7		▷ Respond To Vendor That We Have Prod		Oct 7	Oct 7	1 hour	Recall Manager	5	8
8		▷ Communicate To Inventory Control		Oct 7	Oct 7	1 hour	Recall Manager	7	9
9		▷ Pull Invoices		Oct 7	Oct 8	4 hours	Recall Manager	8	10
10		▷ Locate & Pull Product From Warehouse		Oct 8	Oct 8	4 hours	Inventory Control	9	11
11		▷ Send Comms To Recall Person Product Is Pulled		Oct 8	Oct 8	1 hour	Inventory Control	10	12
12		▷ Communicate Status To Leadership		Oct 8	Oct 8	1 hour	Recall Manager	6; 11	13
13		▷ Communicate Recall Info & Status To Sales		Oct 9	Oct 9	1 hour	Recall Manager	6; 12	14
14		Initial Internal Response Complete		Oct 9	Oct 9			13	15
15		▷ Determine If Product Out For Delivery		Oct 9	Oct 9	1 hour	Recall Manager; Inventory...	14	16; 17
16		▷ IF YES, NOTIFY DRIVERS		Oct 9	Oct 9	2 hours	Transportation	15	18
17		▷ IF NO, ID CUSTOMERS & SHIPMENT		Oct 9	Oct 9	4 hours	Customer Service Rep	15	19; 22
18		▷ Note & Pull From Truck		Oct 9	Oct 10	6 hours	Driver	16	19
19		In-Transit Response Complete		Oct 10	Oct 10			17; 18	

Identify
CONSTRAINTS

From a project management perspective, constraints are restrictions that define a project's limitations. You may be familiar with the concept of the "triple constraint," which refers to scope, schedule, and cost. For the crisis plans you are building, the constraints may be challenging to identify upfront.

Scope—You know that the goal of your plan is to identify tasks that need to be completed in the event of a given crisis. While the scope for each plan is defined, you don't know the actual impact of the crisis, so the scope is loose. You may need to enter additional tasks, or you may be able to skip some of the tasks when executing the plan depending on the situation.

Schedule—You'll create a reasonable timeline based on assumptions. The timeline may change depending on the specific crisis and will become clearer when you are executing your plan. You may not know the schedule until it's go-time, but you know the work, and for now, that's sufficient.

Cost—The constraint around cost will most likely depend on the crisis itself and your specific financial situation at the time of the crisis—which you won't know when the plan is created. So, determine what potential costs could be and create goals to fulfill them. This could come in the form of maintaining a predetermined amount in your savings account or by having a solid insurance policy to cover the costs of your loss. An additional option is business interruption insurance, but it can be costly. This is where a good insurance agent is worth knowing.

You can list constraints directly in your plan, or they can be in a different document entirely. We prefer to list our constraints external to our plan. This approach works for us because we can format in a method that works for us without being confined to a project plan format. For each constraint identified, we listed a risk or impact.

 Turn to **exercise twenty-five** in your book to write down some constraints.

CONSTRAINT	RISK / IMPACT SPACE
RESOURCES: May not have enough staff to handle recall and day-to-day operations	Day-to-day operations will be stretched thin
TIME: We may not be positioned to handle a recall in an appropriate amount of time	Recall may take longer to handle than it should, impacting operations further
QUALITY: Sales team and customer service will be stretched thin	Risk to customer satisfaction as two main teams dealing with customers are now looking specifically at recall issue
SYSTEM: No recall system in place	No automated system allows for human error

Annnnnd...you did it! You completed the last exercise of the book. You earned a drink. (We'll wait here.)

Transparent
COMMUNICATIONS

Here's the deal: You should communicate as much as possible with your employees, customers, vendors, and whoever else needs to stay informed (finance, legal, etc.). By including communications in your plan, you won't "forget" them. The tasks will be right in front of you.

Spend time mapping out the frequency of your communications and the appropriate channel (email, phone calls, social media, etc.). When it's time to execute, a lot of the work is already done. You'll have to craft the messages, but that should be easy: be transparent, answer questions, provide updates. It's important that your communications are two-way and not just you sending out information. It is necessary to respond to the questions and concerns that are coming your way.

How you structure communications in your plan depends on your preference. Here are three suggestions:

- Build a section dedicated to communications in your plan.

- Have an external communications plan that you work from.

- Include communication tasks throughout your plan as needed.

Communication tasks to consider putting in your crisis plan:

- **Initial communication to employees** alerting them to the crisis and what they can expect over the next 24 hours.

- **Initial communication to customers** regarding the crisis and what it means to them. If you don't have a timeline, then be honest about that. Let them know when they will hear more from you and what they can do in the meantime.

- **Initial communication to vendors** informing them of the crisis and the impact to your operations. If you're able to communicate specific information regarding products or services to each vendor, they could potentially offer solutions or options for support.

- **Initial communication to financial institutions, government agencies, etc.** if necessary. You may be able to access available resources or guidance. This is also good to ensure you're within the laws or regulations to avoid penalties and project delays.

- **Regular communications to employees** to keep them informed. Whether that's daily, weekly, or hourly is up to you and dependent upon the scenario, but determine how frequently you will communicate. Then keep that commitment.

- **Follow-up communications to customers, vendors, financial institutions, government agencies, etc.** as necessary. Find a regular cadence to communicate with these groups. As we mentioned earlier, in the absence of information, people fabricate. Don't give anyone a reason to fabricate information.

People's first reaction is going to be "What does this mean for me?" So, tell them what it means for them. Your customer doesn't care about the "why"; they want to know how they will be able to receive the product or service you offer. And, the answer you give may differ for each client. Some may be happy to wait. Others may require an alternative, even if that means going to a competitor.

Corey and Julie:

During the COVID-19 pandemic, one of our clients reached out for help with communications. She owns two yoga studios in central Virginia and she was ready to communicate her reopening strategy to her members. The problem was, she didn't have all of the information about reopening because the Governor hadn't yet released all of the details. But the owner didn't want to wait for all the details because there was no clear date on when information would be available and she wanted to be as transparent as possible with her loyal yoga community.

We worked with the owner to craft an email communication to all of her members that included what they could expect in terms of safety, what the class schedule would look like upon reopening, and what she believed the requirements would be for class size. The communication also included information on membership fees, virtual class offerings, and when a follow-up communication could be expected. She closed by thanking her members for continuing to support her business and provided clear information on how to reach out to her with questions or comments.

She didn't have all of the answers. In fact, she didn't have most of them. But she wanted her customers to know what she knew. The result of a communication that took less than 60 minutes to create? The studios had an uptick in her membership numbers, and the feedback she received was that she was the only studio in the area providing information.

While you may be embarrassed to communicate if the problem is internal, it's still best if you control the messaging. It's better to tell your clients yourself than for them to hear about it on the news or potentially as a second-hand rumor.

We always advise clients that if they get asked a question they can't answer, rather than dodging the question, they should acknowledge their inability to answer. Tell your customers that you can't answer and the reason why (legal, don't have the answer, etc.), and let them know that you will contact them with the answer as soon as possible. You aren't avoiding or lying to them, and you built trust that you are willing to address questions that may not be the most comfortable to answer.

At times, it may feel inappropriate or unnecessary to communicate. While the information to communicate may be situational, being consistent in your messaging will build trust with whoever the audience is for a given message. Reinforce what you do know and be honest about uncertainty whenever possible. If you're in a situation where there may be legal reasons for withholding certain information, and in those instances, it's best to work with your legal counsel to make decisions on what to say and when.

How you communicate during a crisis is critical. Even if you can't answer something directly, acknowledging that you have been asked and that you will come back with an answer is a sign of strong leadership. Don't avoid the hard conversations because they are uncomfortable. Communicating during a crisis is a great time to showcase your leadership.

Tips for
SOLOPRENEURS

In the **CHAPTER 12: CREATE THE PLAN** Tip for Solopreneurs, we discussed the ease of creating a plan when you are the only one who will be managing and executing the plan. Still true. However, also consider that any resource beyond yourself listed in the plan is going to be external so communications need to be on point.

As a solopreneur, consider leveraging additional resources for some tasks when possible. Think about it from this perspective: You're a small business owner who literally does everything yourself. Now you're working through a crisis—that's a lot for one person. Leverage your network, even if it means asking your grandma to help because she's the only person available.

14 REVIEW THE PLAN, KEEP IT CURRENT

"Strength and growth come only through continuous effort and struggle."
—Napoleon Hill, Author

Julie:

I'll admit it. I'm slightly fanatical about well structured, meaningful, and robust project plans. I encourage my clients to include as many details as possible because it makes execution easier. But I also understand that creating a project plan is more art than science. Everyone has their own personal preferences.

A few years back, we were working with a project manager who definitely had his own preferences for creating and maintaining plans. I'm not sure anyone on the team understood what his approach was, but he seemed to have an approach that worked for him.

Well, he was responsible for creating and maintaining a plan for a large-scale IT implementation, and he wasn't well suited for the responsibilities. His plan was disorganized, and he was missing a lot of information. To his credit, he wanted to resolve the gaps in his plan, so he called an ALL-DAY MEETING WITH 30+ PEOPLE to review the project plan, line by line. If your name was listed in the plan, he wanted you in the meeting.

The bulk of the meeting was spent watching him make updates to the plan as he projected his screen for the entire room. Six hours into the meeting his computer crashed. He didn't have auto-save turned on, and he hadn't saved his work since the meeting started.

We could talk about the uprising of an entire team, but that story belongs in a different book.

There are so many tips and tricks I could point out here - but I'll keep it simple. Reviewing plans with the resources doing the work and being respectful of their time is critical for the success of the project. Saving your work as you go is critical for the success of your job.

Review
THE PLAN

You have now built your first draft of a crisis plan. Now spend time reviewing what you have created. Don't worry; it shouldn't take all day to review a single plan.

Reviews can include your entire team, only those roles mentioned in the plan, or yourself and your management team. The key is to review the plan for gaps.

Reviewing allows you to cross-check and ensure that nothing is missing; it also gives those people involved in task execution an opportunity to ask questions. The easiest way to review the plan is to walk through it like it's happening. It's ideal to have all relevant people available, but as we mentioned above, it's not required.

As you complete the review, be sure to update the plan with your findings. That's the whole point.

Keep the
PLAN CURRENT

It's highly unlikely that you will use any of them immediately, so if you're wondering how you're going to keep one plan current—let alone multiple plans—we have some good news: once the plans are created, the maintenance is light.

Unless you eliminate a role or introduce a new critical role (like adding a safety manager to your team), you won't need to make many adjustments to resources within the plan. Most factors will stay the same unless you add or expand, which will require you to review and update your plans.

Big changes in your business should be reflected in the plan, but small changes in day-to-day operations don't necessarily need to be updated. Pick a regular cadence to do a high-level review. Every six months is great, but you should review what you have created at least annually. The plan should be flexible enough that minimal adjustments, if any, can be made easily.

Build additional
PLANS

You will repeat the above for each type of crisis you identified, but the good news is the subsequent plans are much easier to build as the foundation is already there. You can copy from your first plan and reuse as much as possible.

Tips for
SOLOPRENEURS

As a solopreneur you'll still need to review the plans you create. You can accomplish the review by yourself, but we recommend finding someone in your network to work with. Perhaps you and another solopreneur can review each other's crisis plans. That's a great way to expand upon the plans you created.

15 PLANNING RECAP

> "Moral of the story: try to get things right, figure out what's going wrong with the scenario, and don't give up."
> — Cody Lundin, Survival Instructor

Corey:

I was invited to join a group of people in the North Georgia mountains for some outdoor activities. One of those activities was a 28-mile hike/run. Now, I'm not a trail runner by any means. But I do hike often and with a heavy pack, so I didn't think too much about covering 28 miles.

I glanced over the equipment list that was sent and packed "appropriately." I knew going in that it was going to be tough and that I had never traveled that distance on foot in one day before. I'm not in bad shape, but I wasn't in the type of shape required to run that distance. I figured I would "get by."

Well, before the first mile was complete, I was already gassed trying to keep up with the other five people as we made the first ascent up a mountain. Their normal walking gait on an incline was equivalent to a slow jog for me. I didn't even think about how they were all ultra-marathon/trail runner types, with most of them regularly running 50 to 100 miles at a time.

We got to the top and looked across the valley at a ridge line way off in the distance. That was where we were heading. I immediately regretted not preparing myself for this challenge as I realized we were less than a mile into the full 28.

As the day continued, I learned that my running shoes were ill-equipped for trail running, as were my socks. I also learned the selection of food I brought wasn't appropriate for this adventure (there's nothing appetizing about eating a peanut butter bar or jerky while running in the Georgia heat). About the only thing that was appropriate was my water filtration, which I used to filter over 15 liters of water throughout the day.

After nine hours of hiking and running, we made it to the end. I had partially rolled both of my ankles, and I had blisters in between my toes that had been rubbed raw. I could barely walk by the end... but I made it. As awful as that experience was, I ended up getting hooked on the idea of doing it more often. I learned a lot of lessons, and the weekend was a reminder to me of how important it is to plan and prepare.

Review
IT ALL

We covered a lot of ground in **PART II: PLAN** of this book, and we know how challenging it can be to build out plans for something unknown. Here are some tips to remember as you go:

■ Plans can be a combination of step-by-step activities and checklists.

■ If your plans are built around only your critical functions, it's better than nothing. Ideally, you would build plans that cover more detail, but we understand that isn't always possible.

■ Create one plan first and then reuse the applicable parts and pieces it in other plans as you create them.

■ Ask for help. Leverage the people on your team to help you create the plans.

■ If you completed a SWOT as part of this book (which we hope you have) then address the Weaknesses, Opportunities, and Threats before building a plan wherever possible. At a minimum, look to preserve the Strengths as part of your crisis plans.

■ It's best to avoid listing people's names in the plans you're building. List roles instead. This makes the plan more sustainable.

Bottom line: When you're building plans, build them in a manner that makes the most sense for you and your business.

The art of
PLANNING

You are well aware that creating a plan can be complex, it can be high-level, simple, or anything in between. We mentioned early on in **PART II: PLAN** that there aren't a lot of hard rules when it comes to creating plans; it's a matter of finding an approach that is easy to follow and is functional for completing the work.

If you take away only one thing from this book, let it be that having a plan—regardless of the level of detail—is going to be of tremendous value when a crisis hits.

Part III
EXECUTE

16 KNOW YOUR CRISIS

> "If you're acting as a reaction to a really bad situation, it's very easy to make bad decisions quickly."
> — Nick Kokonas, Co-Owner of the Alinea Group

Identify
THE CRISIS

At this point, the planning is done and you should feel secure that you are equipped to handle any critical incident you encounter. Everything you do from now on will be performed during the crisis, so read on and take notes to help when things go south. Regardless of the predicament, stop to think before reacting.

Defining the crisis is the first thing that you should be doing. Ask questions to qualify the potential impact of what you're facing:

- Is it short-term?

- Does it have customer implications?

- Can you still operate your business?

- Have you faced anything like this before?

- Has anyone in your network faced anything like this before?

- Who has been impacted and to what degree?

We cannot emphasize enough that all of the exercises you did throughout this book have helped to prepare you to work through any crisis that comes your way. You'll be able to instinctively make better decisions throughout the crisis, especially early on when things seem chaotic.

You may want to reach out to others in your network or within your local emergency services if they've dealt with anything similar.

Note: If you're dealing with an immediate, real-time emergency such as fire or a tornado, then your response isn't going to be to call others to see what they did. Use your best judgment. (Our attorneys made us put this disclaimer in here.)

Corey:

I volunteer with my local Search and Rescue group, and being CPR certified is a requirement. To stay current, I am required to take the class every other year. Taking the class is repetitive, as are the exercises. The first step a first responder is supposed to perform in any situation is to make sure the scene is safe. It seems like common sense, but they drill that into your head. Enough people have become victims themselves trying to help someone in a dangerous situation that this point is emphasized during every single exercise.

When a disaster strikes, make sure there are no obvious dangers before pulling out your plans.

You're more prepared
THAN YOU THINK

In **PART I: PREPARE,** part of the focus was on knowing yourself, your people, and your customers. The exercises from that section will help you survive a crisis. You completed exercises on your strengths and weaknesses, which will help navigate through whatever predicament being faced. The work completed in **CHAPTER 8: KNOW YOUR PEOPLE** helps you to determine which employees are best suited to jump into action and help with the immediate threat of the critical incident. You also know how to communicate with your customers. Leverage all of that information now.

Many businesses don't have the advantage of preparation going into a crisis, but you do. You already have solutions to problems others don't even if the crisis you're facing appears to be something you've never planned for. You may not have an exact plan for a UFO hitting your building, but if there's a plan for fire, flood, or tornado—all of which would render the building partially unusable—then you have a starting point for that UFO crisis. Grab a plan that closely matches the crisis you're facing and modify it where needed.

Identify what has
BEEN IMPACTED

We have a client, Marty, who owns a custom design and printing shop for things like t-shirts and other apparel. He's been in business for almost a decade with a loyal customer base in the greater Houston area.

While we were working with Marty on a project, his primary t-shirt vendor's employees went on strike. The vendor's operations went from full production to shut down overnight. Marty needed to triage and stabilize his business quickly. He first needed to review inventory and upcoming orders. He had to figure out what he could complete and what could be postponed.

Because Marty relied exclusively on a single-supplier, his entire business was now at risk. He needed to quickly line up another vendor while also assuring his loyal customers that he would continue to meet their needs, delivering the same high-quality products. Marty never anticipated that his vendor wouldn't be able to fulfill his orders, but he did have a plan for supply chain issues since his business had weathered Hurricane Harvey in 2017 and the flooding that came with it. He was able to modify that plan to deal with his current vendor problem.

Triage your
BUSINESS

When you're dealing with a crisis, you have to triage your business to determine what's impacted and to what degree. Don't be overly optimistic during this assessment. Assume the worst-case scenario.

As you assess the situation, identify what needs to be worked first. Not having any sales coming in is bad, but it's also a relatively easy problem to resolve once operations are back up and running (assuming you have an existing customer base). Supply chain issues, on the other hand, can shut down your operations for weeks or months and may not be a problem only you're facing.

How you respond to a crisis that only impacts you will differ from how you respond to a crisis that impacts your entire city, state, or country. A warehouse fire that affects only your warehouse will be treated differently than an earthquake that affects an entire city. Look at each area objectively and think in terms of reaching a resolution. You can sell all day, but if you don't have any product to fulfill those sales, you're solving the wrong problem. Start by addressing the proverbial "axe in the forehead"—those are the immediate concerns. From there, you can build out a list of everything else. You may also realize that something that isn't a problem now may become one soon if it isn't addressed.

After performing the initial triage, you know what the immediate problems are and what can be addressed later.

Corey:

As a part of my Search and Rescue training, I also took a course called "Stop the Bleed." The point of this class is to learn how to stop traumatic bleeding from something like a puncture wound. (They focus mostly on gunshot wounds, but in the woods, I'm more likely to come across someone who accidentally fell on the pointy end of a stick.) We focused on how to get the bleeding to stop because that's the number one threat to someone's life in that situation. Our focus as first responders is keeping them alive long enough to make it to the hospital. Whether or not they get an infection days or weeks later is not our concern.

After you have "stopped the bleeding," you can shift to stabilizing the business. Start by looking at smaller issues that need to be handled. For example, employee and customer communications will need to be addressed quickly. In Marty's scenario, he also needed to figure out if he needed to slow down his sales process. That decision was completely dependent upon his ability to line up a new supplier.

Once stabilization has occurred, you move to damage control. In Marty's scenario, it was dealing with angry customers who may not get their orders fulfilled on time. He had to make calls to all of his customers who could potentially be impacted and figure out solutions for each. A blanket communication wouldn't work as some orders were time-sensitive, while others were no rush.

Again, assess and reassess any tools and resources you have at your disposal. Marty was able to leverage a cousin who sold t-shirts and other apparel. While he had never done business with him before (keeping family and business separate), he did have an avenue he previously hadn't used to help him resolve the supply chain issue. This is a good time to call in or ask for favors.

Be sure you fully understand everything you lost. For Marty, the obvious loss was a supply of shirts, but there was more. He did lose his contract pricing and rebates, so he had to factor this into pricing. Would he continue to make a smaller profit on his apparel? If so, how long could he continue to do so? If he had to work with the new vendor in perpetuity, could he negotiate the same pricing, or would he have to raise his prices? If there was an impact, he needed to have a strategy for how to manage it. On the other hand, he needed to assess if there were opportunities now that he didn't have with his original vendor. When dealing with a crisis or any unexpected change in business, perform a

360-degree evaluation to ensure you have taken advantage of every opportunity.

You should also review the timeliness of what's changing. Is it immediate, or will you have time to create a plan and address potential problems before you see an impact? Having a full understanding of when you'll see impacts can help with the response and overall plan execution.

Finally, can your staff continue to work through the crisis? It's generally best for everyone involved if people can continue to work, but even if employees *can* still work, you should check to see if they need a day or two off as a result of the crisis. People respond very differently to a crisis, so offer support to your team by providing options for when and how they work. If the crisis dictates that you need all hands on deck, be transparent with your team. The more informed they are, the better they will respond.

Control what
YOU CAN

One of the most challenging things about dealing with a crisis for small business owners is the lack of control they have for certain aspects of the crisis. We recommend that you identify what you can and can't control. Here are examples of what you can control:

- Your business's response and your personal response

- Leadership throughout the crisis

- Leveraging your people

- Communications

- Addressing rumors

- Internal processes

Of course, this list is not comprehensive, so brainstorm other aspects that are within your control. If you focus on what you can control, you'll get to the other side of the crisis a much calmer version of yourself. Put your energy into what you can control and be as flexible as possible with everything else. Working through an incident in your small businesses is stressful; there's no reason to make it even more difficult on yourself. Control what you can.

Tips for
SOLOPRENEURS

As a solopreneur, you may think that you're all alone in a crisis, but if you did your homework in the first parts of this book, you would see that you have plenty of people in your network that can help. Be ready to leverage as many of them as possible. This could be your immediate friends and family, or it could even be a temporary hire. It all depends on the situation. The bright side is that some things will be easier since you are the only employee. You can be more nimble and react more quickly than most other businesses. Use that to your advantage.

17 EXECUTE THE PLAN

> "As an entrepreneur, you are constantly playing in uncharted territory, and sometimes things don't work out. That doesn't mean you failed; It just means you may be off course."
> — Jesse Itzler, Entrepreneur

Julie:

I recently attended grown-up camp, and it was amazing—250 adults coming together to share in a common experience. Not to sound like a high school cheerleader, but it was a 'Top 5' experience of my life. Now, if you think we got together and went fishing and hiking during the day and then roasted marshmallows and drank beers around a fire by night, you would be wrong. Granted, there was a fire pit on the first night, and some folks were indulging in beers, but the weekend was more about community, personal development, and challenging ourselves in new ways than it was about campfires and s'mores.

While there were some amazing guest speakers, the main event for the weekend was a four-hour endurance event with the guiding principle of "nobody quits." The camp organizer, Jesse Itzler (entrepreneur, author, and keynote speaker) had created an obstacle course through the woods that was roughly two miles long, and there were portions of the course that were brutal. We started at 8:00 AM and repeated the course for four hours. Nobody quits.

Several months before camp, someone from Jesse's team started sending out weekly training plans to help attendees prepare for the course. I honestly didn't pay any attention to the training. I was doing my own training that at least matched what was being recommended, so I literally had no idea what to expect with the obstacle course.

As we walked the course the day before the event, learning all of the obstacles and seeing the path, I remember thinking to myself, "Oh no, I didn't train enough." But I also remember thinking, "I will not be the one who quits," and thus began an argument in my head that lasted almost 24 hours. There was one particular part of the course that terrified me. I could not sleep thinking about climbing down rock steps to cross over a newly made footbridge. I kept thinking to myself, "You're going to break your leg on those rock steps." I was terrified.

On Saturday morning, as the clock drew closer to start time, I grew more and more anxious. I was surrounded by new friends who kept reaffirming that I was more than capable of completing the four-hour challenge. And they were right. By noon, I had completed 12 miles—more than I had ever completed before. I was damn proud of myself.

And here is what I learned over those four hours: I was more prepared than I thought. No, I didn't complete the exact training plan that Jesse and his team had recommended, but I did complete a training plan. My own. As I looped through that obstacle course, I reminded myself how important it was to have a bias towards action. To keep moving. To do something.

Even if it's only one small step in front of the other, that action makes a difference.

Identify which
PLAN TO USE

In the last chapter, we covered knowing your crisis and focusing on triaging and stabilizing, both of which are vital in any crisis management plan. In this chapter, we are going to talk about executing the plan.

The first thing to do is to identify which plan to use. Regardless of the incident, if you spent time creating plans during **PART II: PLAN,** you have something you can use. It may not match exactly, but it's a starting point.

For now, assume that you have a plan that's an exact match to the crisis. You built a plan for fire, and now you have a fire to deal with. Grab that plan and review it either alone or with your team. The important part is that a high-level review is completed before the start of execution.

Note: this probably doesn't need to be said again—but before reviewing the plan, make sure the fire is actually out.

This review isn't a long process; you have a crisis to deal with, so be as efficient as possible. You're looking for three key things throughout the review:

- Ensure that all the pieces are included in the plan. If anything is missing from the plan, write it down. Start a list of any obvious gaps that may need to be addressed.

- Remove anything from the plan that's unnecessary. Instead of deleting, we recommend moving these tasks out to review them later as they may become relevant once Phase 1—Immediate Action is complete.

- Are all of your listed resources available and/or capable of performing their tasks? If not, assign someone who can complete them.

Chances are that as you begin to execute, instinct will take over. Initially, you'll be moving quickly, so the review will help with having a mental checklist of what needs to happen. Likely, the first handful of tasks will already have been executed before the review even occurs.

If you find yourself dealing with an event for which you don't have a specific plan, do a quick review of your existing plans and find one that treats the same symptoms as your current situation. In **CHAPTER 10: INTRODUCTION TO PLANNING**, we told you the story of the machine shop owner who had a generic plan for a downturn in sales. He planned to reduce hours and work around schedules to keep as many of his staff employed until business picked up again. He hadn't planned for a pandemic, but he had a plan that could fill most of the gaps. It can be that easy.

Now, if you are in a situation where you don't have anything similar, parts of your existing plans may be useful. Once you have started to stabilize, you can most likely leverage parts like communication and normalization tasks. Also, some of your preparations, like having a savings account to cover expenses, can and will likely be utilized during this crisis.

Execute
THE PLAN

Creating a crisis plan is all about strategy. Plan execution should be tactical and is about intentional steps to keep everyone moving and informed. You already completed your internal plan review. Here is a very basic overview of the next steps:

Clarify roles and responsibilities of team members. Everyone needs to know the role they are filling during the crisis.

Collect task updates, issues, risks, and resource constraints. You'll need this information to keep the plan moving forward.

Communicate status updates to stakeholders and team members. Set up predetermined checkpoints where everyone on the team can gather information and ask questions.

Review the upcoming tasks in the plan to confirm everything is still relevant to identify anything that can be completed earlier in the process. Review the plan with external resources, if needed.

If you have determined that someone else is leading the execution of the crisis plan, you should clarify roles and responsibilities for the entire team. Your team needs to be clear about what they can expect from you versus the person leading the plan execution. In **THE LEADERSHIP YOUR COMPANY NEEDS DURING A CRISIS** section of **CHAPTER 7: KNOW YOURSELF,** we discussed clearly defining leadership during a crisis to avoid confusion. Take a few minutes to review that section to refresh your memory. Now's the time to communicate with your team, so there is no confusion.

Whoever is leading the crisis will also need a method for receiving task updates from the assigned resources. It's not only important for whoever is leading to communicate to the team, but the team needs to communicate back when tasks are completed. You learned in **PART II: PLAN** that in some situations, certain tasks cannot begin until other tasks have been completed; therefore, receiving task updates is critical to keep moving the plan forward. Keep the communication lines open.

During plan execution, everyone must be informed of progress. Whoever is leading the execution should be the one communicating to the team. Holding check-ins at designated times will ensure that all involved are on the same page.

It would not be unusual to see hourly conference calls initially if the crisis is big enough and things are moving very quickly. However, the frequency of the updates (hourly, daily, etc.) will depend upon the severity of the crisis. As you move further along in the execution and are heading towards stabilization, the frequency can be reduced.

The important thing is to communicate status. Status can come in a variety of formats. It can be communicated via conference calls, in-person meetings, emails, or even text messages. We have personally been involved in numerous projects where a combination of all has been used.

In addition to your internal team, review the plan with the necessary external support resources identified in **CHAPTER 8: KNOW YOUR PEOPLE.** You will need to provide clear and concise information on what is happening, what you plan to do, and what to expect.

Pivot your
BUSINESS

It's easy to find examples of pivots if you think about how businesses responded to COVID-19. Many businesses, large and small, had to pivot their models for survival while others pivoted to produce products that were in short supply. Gyms and fitness studios began offering virtual classes. Restaurants were forced to pivot toward an online and curbside-only experience while some distilleries decided to change their production lines to hand sanitizer instead of booze. Hair salon owners started selling "at-home color kits" that offered clients their exact color formula in a single-use kit.

Pivots occur when a business is adjusting to some negative event or when a new opportunity exists. Pivots can be short-lived, or they can be a permanent change to your business model. The pivots we're talking about in this book are ones you haven't planned for; they are an adjustment based on an unforeseen situation. And as you've already learned in this book, the most effective way to implement change is to create a plan and execute against it.

But before throwing this book to the other side of the room and stomping off because there's another plan to create, give us a minute to explain. These aren't going to be the long, drawn-out, detailed plans you created earlier. These are high-level plans created on the fly. Keep reading!

The goal of this section is to help prepare you to make pivots during a crisis. The intention isn't to pick this book up during a crisis to figure out what to do next.

Consider how the businesses discussed above chose to pivot. Now, how would you approach pivoting your business during a crisis?

To create a plan, you need to know what you are planning for. That's the first rule of a good plan: have a goal. What is the pivot you are making? Ask yourself some questions to narrow down your options. Here is a list of examples to get you thinking:

- What parts of my business are currently operating?

- Are there any new restrictions or regulations on what I can do?

- Is there anything in my business model that I wanted to change but haven't had a chance to? It makes sense to look at this now, because the timing may be perfect for making a change you've been putting off.

- Do I have any feedback from customers or employees that I can group together and then act on?

- Is there a way to shift my product or service to a different format or location? What would changing locations entail? How easily could you change formats?

- Is there a different target market I need to focus on during this crisis? Who is that market and why would you shift your focus to them? Would this shift be temporary or long-term?

You may have a few options for pivoting your business, so you may need to prioritize them to determine the best course of action. You can prioritize based on several different factors:

- Ease to implement

- Increased revenue

- Customer request

- Ease to unpivot

The factor you use to prioritize may differ based on the crisis at hand. You may need to consider any restrictions that could prevent you from making the pivot.

Now that you have prioritized, it's safe to assume that #1 on your list is the pivot you are going to make for your business. You know what's next, right? Creating a plan. It's okay to keep this simple and create a plan using a checklist. It's fast and easy. Here is what your checklist should include:

- List of tasks to complete

- An owner for each task

- A timeline for each task

Now that you have a checklist or maybe even a formal plan, it's time to dig a little deeper into the details.

Will the pivot you're making result in any broken processes? For example, will there be a disruption in the supply chain because you now need to order additional products that you didn't previously order? Will you need to change the way you are interacting with your customers? At the very minimum, spend a few minutes reviewing your most critical end-to-end processes and ensure that nothing will be broken. You still want to deliver the same great service to your customers.

Don't forget how important communication is, so make sure to include that in your pivot plan. You can always reuse your communication tasks from previous plans.

Assess *if a pivot is*
THE RIGHT MOVE

Before you move forward with a pivot, pull back and look at it from another direction. Have you fully considered the benefit the pivot would provide? You know something needs to happen, but is this the "something" that will get you there? Is there any chance that this pivot could hurt your business? Would it tarnish your brand in any way?

While we fully support the need to pivot, we also recognize that pivots can be tough to execute in the middle of a crisis. Sometimes the best course of action you can take is to wait and see. You don't want to give your employees and customers whiplash by trying something new every single day. While we cover pivoting your business and adjusting on the fly, there's also value in maintaining steady-state as much as possible. It gives you time to make informed decisions.

Crisis creates opportunity. That opportunity comes in many different forms, and you should be looking for ways to take advantage of those opportunities. If a pivot works well you may want to make the change permanent. Track what worked well or didn't work, and be prepared to make changes to your business model and other crisis plans, based on what you learn.

18 HANDLE THE REST

"I'm going to use this to my advantage. I'm going to take what my competition does and do it better. I'm going to put them out of business and burn their businesses to the ground. It's the Viking approach to merchant services."
— Zak Allmand, Owner at Apex Payment Solutions

While we don't encourage you to gain a competitive advantage over your competition by literally burning them to the ground, we love the spirit of the above quotation. But we do have a story about how an actual business fire was handled:

Corey:

I used to be a partner in a small chain of coffee shops, and I got a call one day from one of my managers that one of our buildings was on fire. Our shop occupied the ground floor of a four-story building, and it was actually one of the apartments above us that was burning.

The fire department did a great job of putting the blaze out quickly, but since we were below the apartment, all of the water used to put out the fire drained into our space. We had a plan we could leverage as we had dealt with a hurricane a few years prior, but we still had to make changes on the fly. We were able to move the undamaged inventory to our other stores, and our insurance covered the clean-up costs. However, keeping the employees of the affected store busy and paid during this time wasn't something we had factored in.

One quick solution was to schedule some of the staff to help clean up and prepare the store for reopening, while other team members approached it as a surprise vacation. We were able to move the rest of the staff to our other stores as some of the employees at those locations voluntarily gave up their shifts to take some time off as well.

Act with
CONFIDENCE

By this point in the crisis, you should be well on your way to stabilization, but you can't flip to autopilot—you have to be ready to react. Start working on the less than critical problems, but be sure you're still protecting your strengths.

Start by looking at problems you triaged earlier in the process but did not address at the time. Prioritize those and begin addressing them. As you executed the plan, you likely found some gaps. Only Hannibal from the A-Team can create a gap-free plan, so don't beat yourself up. Take the time to update the plan and fill in the gaps. You never know when this plan may need to be used again.

Most importantly, continue to lead confidently. Even though things are starting to normalize, you want your team to remain vigilant and to understand the big picture. Lead everyone through this crisis.

Big Benefit of
BEING SMALL

If there's one benefit to being a small business owner, it's that you generally have more flexibility than the big guys do.

It's never a surprise to anyone when America goes to war. There is no sneak attack. We have to move enormous amounts of resources that can be easily tracked, not to mention the fact that social media and the news broadcast everything that's going on. But, you aren't a large, imposing military. You're small. You're a ninja. Use that to your advantage.

What this means is you can adjust your plans quickly with little issue. Tweaking the plan as you go is completely fine, but this isn't a license to be arrogant about your planning, or lack thereof. Meaning, don't assume that because you're small, you can get away without a plan. If this book hasn't taught you the importance of a plan, go back to **CHAPTER 1: THE FOUNDATION** and start over. You're better than that.

You aren't a superhero,
AND THAT'S OKAY

Even without a crisis happening, there is a ton of work to be done on a daily basis when you own a small business. Now throw a crisis on top of it, and the work can feel insurmountable at times. When it feels like it's too much, we can't say it enough: Ask for help! That can be from anyone in your business, community, or even your customers. When you're in the thick of it all, it's helpful to get a fresh, outside perspective of your situation.

Some crises you go through as a community and crises you go through alone as a business. The COVID-19 pandemic was a community crisis. Businesses—even competitors—leaned on one another to come up with solutions, and some even partnered to combine services. This may have been you. Other times you're going through a crisis alone, and you're not sure who to ask for help.

Regardless of the situation, you aren't unique. Others have been through something similar and can offer help. It's okay to ask for help, and it's okay not to know all of the answers. You're going to make mistakes along the way, and that's to be expected. You're in uncharted territory, so mistakes mean you're trying something new. If you make a mistake, own it, and move on.

It takes a strong person to admit that they don't know something. True strength is not having all of the answers, nor is it doing all of the work yourself; true strength is admitting you don't know what to do and then asking for help. Sometimes it's hard to make that admission when you have a team of employees depending on you. Don't worry about what others think of how you run your business. It's far more important to stay in business than it is to have people think you're Superman.

Find a way to keep track of the decisions made and the changes implemented. At the moment, you'll say to yourself, "I don't need to write this down because I'm never going to forget this stuff," but you will. You'll forget. Write it down.

All of this is a learning opportunity, and it's going to make you a stronger business owner and leader.

Grow as A LEADER

First and foremost, continue to lead with confidence. Your team and customers have stuck with you through the crisis, and that wasn't an accident. That was a choice. You took deliberate action and you executed a preexisting plan to get back to normal as quickly as possible.

Your leadership style is a reflection of your business. Think about how you view your competition: you know when they are making decisions because they are scared versus when they are making moves from a position of power. That's how to lead when you're taking your business from surviving, to maintaining, to thriving.

Opportunities to learn new things will be everywhere as you go through a crisis. You'll find out how well you communicate, how well you plan, and how loyal your employees and customers are. You'll learn every day, and it won't always be fun. But, as a small business owner, you already know the challenges that come daily.

We promise this is the last time we'll mention this, but we really want to drive the point home:

Communicate confidently to your employees and customers. You have already gotten them through the crisis; now you're leading them through change. In theory, that's easier.

One of the single best things to do through this process is to encourage your staff to grow with you. Chances are if you have employees, most of them haven't been through anything like this before; therefore, providing them with the opportunity to grow and develop new skills is a tremendous opportunity in itself. Learning from a leader who has taken them through a crisis and is now making moves to grow the business is a big deal. As an employee, these are the moments that people carry with them for the rest of their careers. The more you communicate about why decisions were made and the impact of those decisions, the more you are building strong leaders within your team. Think about that the next time you face a crisis.

19 POSTMORTEM

Execution review and **IDENTIFICATION OF GAPS**

If you look back over the work done in this book and how it prepared you for surviving a crisis, you should feel incredibly proud. It wasn't easy to get this far. Honestly, the planning part of the book is like a climb up Mount Everest: it doesn't seem to end. But here you are, you made it through the crisis. It's probably a good time to stop, breathe, and reflect on which parts of this process were easy and which were difficult and caused you to struggle. Where could you make adjustments?

If another crisis hit next week, would you be good with the plans you have? What did you learn through this crisis that you could document, even if only in a bulleted list so that things are easier next time?

What worked well from your planning and execution? How did your employees respond and execute? Did your customers feel informed? Did you lose customers throughout the process? What caught you off guard?

It's important to reflect on what worked and what didn't. There's an opportunity in what didn't work—and that opportunity is in being better prepared for future events.

The reality is, you don't know if there will be a next time, but if you have learned anything in this book, it's far better to be even a little prepared than it is to wing it during a crisis.

Corey and Julie:

Our research process for this book coincided with the early weeks of the COVID-19 shutdown, and while there are a lot of negatives that happened as a result of the shutdown, there were some benefits. Chiefly, it provided businesses with an opportunity to reflect on how they prepare for emergencies, albeit a little too late. Over 80% of the businesses we interviewed for this book told us they were "lucky" when it came to being prepared for shutting down their businesses. Lucky?

Having 3-6 months of expenses in savings, a clear employee and customer communication strategy, and potential pivots lined up for your business isn't "lucky." That's called being prepared. Granted, none of them had ever envisioned a world in which a pandemic would shut their business down for weeks on end, but most of them had some type of plan they could follow. That's what we mean by creating a plan and knowing that it doesn't have to be perfect. It only needs to exist with key tasks.

If you could go back in time before a crisis, what would you have done differently? This is the question to ask after surviving one. You can now do a postmortem on the actual plan and execution and find ways to improve. Again, we recognize that you have a business to run, so you don't have a lot of time to be creating and recreating plans, but ideally, you have enough time for a 60-minute meeting to get input from your team on what worked well and what can be improved for the future.

Finally, take a look at what opportunities emerged that you didn't plan for. Hopefully, this is where you have the most data to work with because that means your plan to recover from the crisis was solid.

Prepare for
NORMALCY

This is the point where you should be ready for operations to return to normal. By now, you should have identified everything that has changed within your business. You will need to ensure that any pivots you made are documented and accounted for in any future or existing planning.

You should also have a plan for any unpivots that are needed. It's highly unlikely that everything you adjusted during the crisis will remain in play, so have a plan and the timeline for when the unpivot(s) will occur.

An unpivot plan doesn't have to be overly complex. A document listing details in sequential order will likely suffice. Turn to the planning section of the book and give yourself a refresher on creating a plan. The more you create them, the more second nature the process will become.

Finally, think about communications and if there's anything additional to share. This includes communicating with your employees, customers, and external team. Depending on how long you were operating in crisis mode, it may help to inform everyone that things are now back to normal. We will never stop reinforcing the need for strong communication.

Tips for
SOLOPRENEURS

Since it's only you, be sure to document, document, document! And do so immediately, so you don't forget.

CONCLUSION

"Strength does not come from winning. Your struggles develop your strengths. When you go through hardships and decide not to surrender, that is strength."
— Arnold Schwarzenegger, Actor

We know how hard it is to run a small business. But doing hard things builds strength and resilience, and those are two of the characteristics required to be successful. As a small business owner, you must continuously be in bold pursuit of your goals. Owning a business is not for the faint of heart, and honestly, preparing yourself and your business to survive a crisis isn't either.

If history has taught us anything, it's that people have short memories. As much as we would love to believe that every business owner in America will be prepared the next time a crisis hits, it's extremely unlikely. People forget regardless of the size of their business. We had a financial crisis in 2008 that should have taught every business person to have cash reserves in the event of an economic downturn. But when the COVID-19 pandemic hit, we learned quickly that businesses were not set to survive.

While we've primarily focus on you creating a crisis plan, the underlying message of this book is about positioning your small business better. By helping you find ways to increase revenue and build better relationships with your customers and employees, we hope to help you make your business the strongest it can be.

Seriously? Now What?! is filled with opportunities for every small business owner. We hope that you continue to take advantage of everything you learned from reading this book and completing the exercises. There is value in continuing to use these tools as your business grows.

Let's work together to strengthen small businesses. Let's do the hard work and be prepared for anything that comes our way.

To quote John Connor in *Terminator II: Judgment Day*: "The future is not set. There is no fate but what we make for ourselves."

Hasta la vista, baby.

ACKNOWLEDGMENTS

Writing a book was a new and challenging experience for us. This book would not have been possible without the generosity of so many people who willingly gave their time, experience, and support throughout the whole process.

First, we have to thank Jim House who worked with us from the beginning, helping us map out the content, working with us on voice, approach, and distribution, and answering our countless questions. *Throughout the process you kept the train on the tracks, Jim.*

Second, we have to thank our editor Vanessa L. Ruccolo. Having someone read and edit your work can be sensitive, but Vanessa made the process enjoyable. She was able to offer feedback without raising our defenses, helping us to craft the best book possible. We actually enjoyed reading through her comments because she would surprise us with quotes from *The Office, Arrested Development, and The Simpsons. Vanessa, you have a true talent for putting people at ease during difficult situations.*

To our families and friends for understanding that our availability over the past four months was significantly reduced while we worked long days to meet our deadlines. *Thank you to each of you for supporting us on this crazy adventure and regularly reminding us to keep going when the process was hard.*

Thank you to Carmen Sima who brilliantly designed our book cover, workbook, and so much more. *Carmen, you are amazingly talented and we will forever be grateful for crossing paths with you.*

To Jennifer Lazarus, the best marketing guru we've ever worked with. *Jen, from day one you made us better and we will never understand how we got so lucky to work with you.*

Thank you Jenn Mallory for making us look good (literally!) in our head shots. You made the session fun, your eye for detail was incredible, and you gave us mimosas to help us smile. *You're the best photographer we know Jenn!*

To Michael Edmondson: Thank you for giving us guidance on how to structure the book. *The feedback and information you provided made our book better and the process easier.*

Fionn Ó Cathaláin: We found you on the Internet, and you batted cleanup on our final draft. *You called us on our stupid writing habits and made the book "actually" better.*

Adam Carolla and Andy Frisella: We don't know you personally (yet), but we are so thankful you have the platforms you do. *You're both quoted more in our daily lives than any other individuals.*

Finally, and most importantly, to the small business owners who participated in our research: You are the reason we wrote this book. Your tenacity and desire to keep pushing forward, no matter the circumstances, are exactly what it means to be a small business owner.

- Zak Allmand of Apex Payment Solutions
  (www.apexpaymentsolutions.com)

- Camille Bird of Sacred Waters Spa, Richmond, VA

- Bill Bolton of BB Insurance, Leesburg, VA
  (www.bbinsurancehub.com)

- Harry Boyd of Virginia Museum of Fine Arts, Richmond, VA

- Suzanne Burns of Humble Haven Yoga, Richmond, VA

- Michele and George Ceniviva of Orangetheory Fitness,
  Audubon and Collegeville, PA & Ceniviva's Precision
  Paving & Concrete, Willow Grove, PA

- Bob Dalsimer of Inspira Group, Orange County, CA

- Barbara DeCost of Miller's Hill Farm, Farmville, VA

- Kaui Garcia and Colby Martin of Keller Williams, Chester
  County, PA

- Brenda Gore of The Gore Benefits Group, Raleigh, NC

- Jesse Harris of East Coast Endodontics, Richmond, VA

- Jason Klehr of Northwest Automatics, Inc., Kent, WA

- Ross Liggett of Metolius Golf
  (www.metoliusgolf.com)

- Aaron Marks of Marks Family Dentistry, Richmond, VA

- Niki Miller of Decks and Beyond Troy, OH

- Stephanie Pearson of PearsonRavitz
  (www.pearsonravitz.com)

- Noah Pines of Ross and Pines, LLC, Atlanta, GA

- Matt Reese of Blk Ankr Originals, LLC, Annapolis, MD

- Paul Santos of Visual Chefs, Richmond, VA

- Melissa Stevens of Purdy & Co., Henderson, MN

- Amy Stevens Tucker of Salty Britches (www.getsaltybritches.com)

- Jake Thompson of Compete Every Day (www.competeeveryday.com)

- Heather Vargo of Life Guidance Associates, Paoli, PA

- Gary Walker of Cabo Fish Taco (www.cabofishtaco.com)